"A bagel bible—a fun read!"
Larry King, USA *Today*

"The Bagels' 'Veggie Bagel' is as good for dinner or a late afternoon snack as it is for Sunday morning noshing."
The *Washington Post*

"Just because your name is Bagel, do you have the right to write a book about them? Yes, if you do as witty, thorough a job as Marilyn and Tom Bagel have done."
Los Angeles Herald Examiner

Photo: Jan Roy

A typical day with Marilyn and Tom Bagel . . .The Bagels, noted for their cooking and imaginative entertaining, know there's more to bagels than cream cheese!

D0521717

The art of bageling:

1. taking doughnut-shaped rolls of delectable flavor and consistency and having lots of fun in the kitchen.

2. I bagel. You bagel. They bagel. "Want to bagel?"

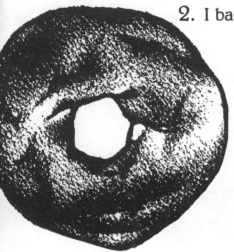

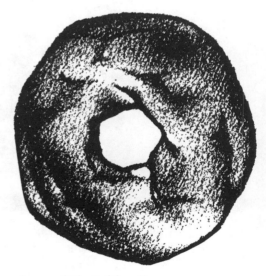

"We never met a bagel we didn't like."

Marilyn and Tom Bagel

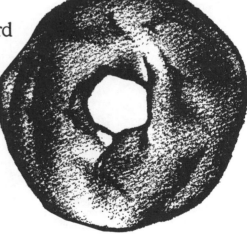

The Bagel Book

by Marilyn & Tom Bagel
(no kidding!)

Illustrations by Donna Ward

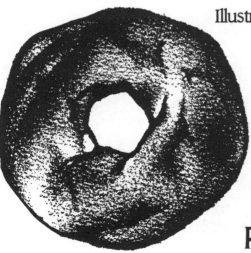

Poppyseed Press

Bethesda, Maryland

Contents

*Our book is dedicated with love
to our parents,
Evy & Aaron Modance
and Alice & Ernst Bagel.
And to our son, Alan,
and our daughter, Florrie.*

Poppyseed Press
4807 Bethesda Avenue, Suite 156, Bethesda, MD
20814

For additional copies of *The Bagel Book,* **send check
or money order for $7.95 plus $1.50 to cover postage
and handling for each book to: Poppyseed Press,
4807 Bethesda Avenue, Suite 156, Bethesda, MD
20814.**

**Inquire about our special quantity discounts with
bulk purchase.**

Library of Congress Catalog Number: 89-504 27

ISBN 0-926990-00-4

Chapter 10

Celebrity Bagels   *What's What With the "Who's Who"*   **103**

Acknowledgements

To Marty and Jo-Anne Modance

To the official members of our Bagel Board: Renée Channey Gabriel and Arnold D. Gabriel, Jan Roy, Resa Messinger.

To Bonnie Hershberg for a lifetime of love.

To my dear friend, Norman Broad—the day we met changed my life.

To Linda Wright for tackling a mechanical nightmare and winning.

To Michael Kaplan for his willingness, friendship and wonderful cover design.

To Peter Garfield for joining the bagelholics and saying "yes" to doing the cover photography.

Growing Up as a Bagel

Some parents have boys. Some have girls. My mother gave birth to two bagels. My parents, Ernst and Alice, told me and my brother Bob what our name "Bagel" meant—a Jewish hard roll. But growing up as a Lutheran boy in Milwaukee, I never had the experience of tasting a bagel. It wasn't until 1968 when I was out of college and in the business world that I had the opportunity at Eagerman's in Boston to meet my namesake and enjoy my first bagel.

One bagel and *this* Bagel was hooked! Compared to ordinary bread, there was no contest; bagels became the bread of life for me. It wasn't long before I was a bagel-holic. I couldn't stop eating them—they were so terrific! Because I didn't care all that much for lox or plain cream cheese, I began to experiment with other ways to enjoy my bagels. Most people seemed to be satisfied with the status quo—bagels and cream cheese, bagels and butter, bagels and lox with a slice of tomato. I soon knew from experience there was much much more to a bagel ....

When I moved to New York in 1969, I found that being a Bagel was like having the key to the city. I could go into any bagel bakery in town, pull out my American Express Card and say, "Do you know who I am?" I'd get special service, free bagels—the works!

Since that day in Boston when I savored my very first bagel, I've consumed literally thousands and thousands of bagels from New York to Miami to Los Angeles. As a third generation Bagel, I can say with absolute authority: Everything's better with a Bagel!

Tom Bagel

I Now Pronounce Me Bagel and Wife.

Some people marry doctors. Some marry lawyers. I married a Bagel, and with the words "I do," became one too! Though I had been a bagel-lover from birth, instant Bagel-dom required a bit of adjustment. (Like getting used to repeating my name because people never believe it the first time around.) I also quickly discovered that everyone has a favorite bagel one-liner. A business client even suggested that I give my name a French twist, accenting the last syllable and pronouncing it "Bagelle"!

In doing research for this book, we'd phone bagel bakers and manufacturers, leave our name, and they'd always think we were crank callers. Some people even asked us if we had changed our name to match the book!

But I have to say, as one of the very few living, breathing Bagels in the world, I have Bagel Pride in my official "roll." First of all, nothing beats two creative Bagels in the kitchen. Plus, as a VIB (Very Important Bagel), I get instant service and immediate attention in bagel stores and delicatessens everywhere! Besides, no one ever forgets my name, it's a great conversation starter, *and* I'm universally loved. Everyone loves a Bagel.

So, however many times you ask me if my father's name is Poppyseed, or if I have a sister named Cinnamon, or if you tell me not to get too much sun because I could become a toasted Bagel, I'll answer with a smile. Especially if you ask me what my favorite kind of bagel is. That's an easy one—Tom Bagel!

Marilyn Bagel

Chapter 1

Bagel Awareness
Basic Bagel Roots

Bagels *should* be found in the dictionary under "fun," but according to Webster (though we haven't been able to determine how he preferred *his* bagels), a bagel is defined as:

> ba•gel \ bāgəl\n.[Yiddish *beygel*, from (assumed) Middle High German *böugel* (whence German dial. *beugel, bäugl*), diminutive of Middle High German *boug-, bouc* ring, bracelet, from Old High German *boug; bheug* (to swell; with derivatives referring to bent, pliable, or curved objects); akin to Old English *bēag, bēah* ring, bracelet, Middle English *bege]:* a hard roll shaped like a doughnut that is made of raised dough and cooked by simmering in water and then baked to give it a glazed brown exterior over a firm white interior.

A Look at Bagel Genealogy

There are practically as many versions of the origin of bagels as there are bagels themselves.
For instance...

Legend has it that in 1683 in Vienna, Austria, a local Jewish baker wanted to thank the King of Poland for protecting his countrymen from Turkish invaders. He made a special hard roll in the shape of a riding stirrup—"beugel," in Austrian—commemorating the king's favorite pastime, and giving the bagel its distinctive shape.

When bagels reached Poland, they were officially sanctioned as gifts for women in childbirth and mentioned in the Community Register. Mothers used them as nutritious teething rings which their infants could easily grasp.

Finding their way to Russia, bagels—called ''bubliki''—were sold on strings in Russian towns. As with other circular objects, they were said to bring good luck and possess magical powers. It is even said that songs were sung about bagels!

Ellis Island and Beyond

When the Jewish immigrants arrived in America, so did the bagel. Today, however, bagels are not just an ethnic food. They're an *everybody* food!

The U.S. bagel industry put down formal roots in New York between 1910 and 1915 with the formation of the Bagel Bakers Local # 338. This select group of 300 craftsmen who had bagels in their blood limited new members to sons of members, who worked in 36 union bagel shops in New York City and New Jersey.

Know-how and back-breaking strength were their stock in trade. Men were paid by the piece and usually worked in 3-man teams. Two made the bagels, one baked, and a ''kettleman'' was in charge of boiling them— one of the most distinguishing characteristics of bagel making. The men each earned about 19¢ a box; each box typically contained 64 bagels. It was not unusual for a team to make 100 boxes a night.

Bagel makers' sons apprenticed for months to learn the trade. In the late 50's and 60's, New York and New Jersey's bagel specialists migrated to other parts of the country. One such bagel veteran, Jack Rubenstein, who learned the art of bagel making at his father's knee, opened Bagel Master Inc. with partner Jack Singer in a suburb of Washington, D.C. It was 1966 when he first signed the lease, and he remembers his landlord had serious doubts. ''Who's gonna spend 7¢ for one of *those* things?'', he asked.

Other bagel bakers who emigrated from Eastern Europe settled in Canada and helped cities like Toronto and Montreal earn their reputations for superb bagels.

Pre-packaged bagels were introduced in grocery stores in the 1950's and the availability of frozen bagels in the 60's enabled consumers to have access to bagels even if they were not near bagel bakeries.

Bagel-making machines, a boon to commercial bakers, were introduced in the early 60's. Inventor Dan Thompson says, "I was born to invent a bagel machine. My father was thinking about a bagel-making machine when I was conceived." That may not be far from the truth, because Dan's father had a wholesale bakery in Winnipeg, Canada, and was already working on a bagel-making machine back in 1926. But it was far too complicated, too slow, too costly to make, and not commercially feasible. There were as many as 50 unsuccessful attempts to produce a bagel making machine in the early 20th century. Dan Thompson's Thompson Bagel Machine Corporation developed the first viable one, despite "doubting Thompsons" who said, "No machine will ever replace the human hand." Most of the early machines were leased by bakers who paid by the dozen on a running time-meter. Now most are purchased. One model can form 200 dozen bagels an hour, another as many as 400 dozen an hour.

Today, the bagel business is "rising" as fast as its yeast, and not just from relatives born into the business. Prominent corporate names are putting their "dough" in it, and bagel marriages occur in boardrooms as liaisons are made between major bagel bakers and the country's leading grocery chains. A far cry from bagel pushcarts on cobblestone streets at the turn of the century! And a great opportunity for bagel lovers to enjoy all the competition heating up.

Chapter 2

Bagel Etiquette
The Hole Truth

A Special Message to the Uninitiated and the Bagel Novice

Are you intimidated by bagels? Do you pass up the bagel section of your grocery store in favor of the bread shelf?

Or, if you do buy a bagel or two, do you ask that they be put in plain brown wrappers...

Or worse yet, try to pass them off as doughnuts?

Fear no more. You're about to help stamp out bagel illiteracy. Welcome to Basic Bagel 101, with THE BAGEL BOOK your only required reading. You are now well on your way to becoming a graduate Bagelologist!

Some of us can trace our bagel fears back to childhood and being raised in a bagel-less household. Others may have experienced specific bagel trauma as an adult. A friend of ours went to lunch with a colleague, ordered a bagel and cream cheese, put the halves together like a sandwich, and began to eat it, whereupon she was informed that one *never* eats a bagel except in separate halves. We have, however, extensively researched both the Old and New Testaments, and have found no eleventh commandment to that effect.

A Word to the Bagel-Wise

Anything you can do with bread, you can do with a bagel, and more. In other words, "a jug of wine, a bagel, and thou..." is where it's at. What's more, bagels are never dull, like a slice of boring white bread just lying there on a plate. Bagels have personality! They sit up tall and proud and golden brown, waiting to be sliced, spread, topped, or scooped out and filled. And let's get something straight. There is no "right way" or "wrong way" to eat bagels. Any way you slice it, bagels are a delicious experience. Besides, as bagel veterans will tell you, what better way to go around in circles?

The Birth of the Bagel

Bagels are made in a unique way that gives them a distinctively chewy texture—one you can really sink your teeth into. Yet a good bagel is tender enough so you don't leave your teeth behind. After the dough is mixed and shaped into circles, it is boiled—"kettled"—before it is baked, which gives the finished bagels their shine.

Before they're popped into the oven, the drained bagels can be brushed with beaten egg, though this step is usually eliminated by professional bakers. Each bagel bakery has its own special "Double-O Bagel" top-secret recipes and techniques that result in the delightful variations to be found across the country.

But wherever you buy your bagels, you'll never see "bagel holes" for sale. Unlike doughnuts, there are no leftover holes in the bagel shaping process, whether it is done by hand or machine. When bagels are made by hand, the dough is either formed into ropes and pressed together at the ends, or shaped into balls whose centers are pushed through and widened with the fingers.

Bagels vary in size from baker to baker and manufacturer to manufacturer; they range in weight from 2 ounces to more than 5 ounces. The average is about 3½ ounces. Bagelettes (miniature bagels) weigh about 1 ounce each.

Bagelmania

You can find bagels and bagelettes in your grocery at the bakery counter, in the bread section, at the deli counter, in special bins or displays, and in the freezer section, as well as at bagel bakeries, convenience stores, and even department stores. In fact, bagel bakeries have the distinction of their very own section in the Yellow Pages of many telephone directories. So if you're on a bagel-hunting expedition, let your fingers do the leg-work for you. In fact, some cities feature bagel bakeries that are open 24 hours a day for the true bagel-holic.

You can eat bagels toasted, heated, or fresh from the bag. If you buy your bagels at a bagel bakery, where they're being baked continuously, you'll often have the good fortune to get them hot from the oven. And because you won't be able to resist the indescribable aroma of fresh bagels, you'll find yourself reaching into the bag on the way home. So be sure to buy a few extra for the road!

Mmmmmmm

Bagels come in an amazing assortment of flavors. The basic plain bagel is frequently called a "water bagel." An "egg bagel" (also a plain version), has a slightly yellow color because it contains eggs. But these are only the beginning. Bagels come in deliciously wonderful variations, including onion, garlic, poppyseed, sesame seed, salt, pumpernickel, rye, cinnamon-raisin, wheat, and honey-wheat. We've found some really unusual flavors at creative bagel bakeries, including banana-nut, cheese, English muffin, cherry, blueberry, chocolate chip and, in California, even jalapeño bagels. Bagel bakeries also sell bags of bagel chips—very thin bagel slices that have been baked crunchy brown. They are the baker's solution to day-old bagels and are great with dips, soups, as the Bagel Nachos we'll tell you how to make, or for just plain munching.

Another Crust of Bagel Knowledge

You've heard of the gold standard, but did you know there's a bagel standard? Because the U.S. bagel industry had its roots in New York City, where so many of the European bakers settled, New York bagels are often considered bagel nirvana and the standard by which all other bagels should be measured. Moreover, the excellent quality of New York water enhances both the taste and the crust. Many of the bagel bakers we spoke with whose bakeries lie outside the New York area use water filtration systems, especially those located in highly chlorinated locales.

Incidentally, you may see ads or store signs that say, ''We have New York bagels.'' That doesn't necessarily mean they use water from New York, or that they ''import'' the dough from Brooklyn. It just means they think their bagels are tops!

The more aggressive bagel purveyors sometimes engage in friendly ''Bagel Wars,'' in which bakers armed with special recipes, techniques, and claims battle over who bakes the best bagels in town. The more varieties you try as you make your way along bagel road the sooner you'll discover *your* favorite brands, bakers, and flavors. Have a wonderful trip!

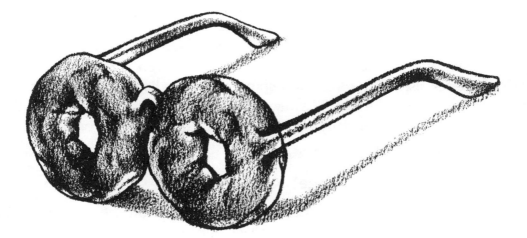

Chapter 3

Special Occasion Bagels
Don't Be Afraid to Ask!

Any bagel maker worth his salt can make up special-order bagels for you. Our family recently enjoyed a "bagel birthday cake"—a giant 16" cinnamon-raisin bagel prepared for us by a bagel bakery. We used a cake decorating kit to write "Happy Birthday" and then topped it off with birthday candles to make it official. It made a big hit and was absolutely delicious, especially with piping hot cups of cinnamon-flavored coffee. We ended up freezing the leftover "cake" and enjoying it again and again as we defrosted pieces in the oven.

Savvy bagel bakers like being one step ahead of their customers when it comes to holiday seasons. You can get green bagels—(what else?)—for St. Patrick's Day, and cherry-flavored pink ones for Valentine's Day. Both make fun gifts to take to friends. Some bakeries even take special orders for heart-shaped bagels, a romantic favorite of ours.

You can also order giant bagels from bakeries, and have them filled with an assortment of meats, cheeses, and coleslaw, or lox, cream cheese, whitefish and tomatoes, or whatever intriguing combination your heart desires. Use our recipes to fire your imagination, and think bagel-liberation! It's an absolutely great way to entertain a crowd!

Chapter 4

The Bagel-On-The-Street Survey

Because even we must acknowledge that one cannot live by bagels alone, we surveyed a cross-section of people—aged 4 to 74—to determine the true dimensions of bagelmania. Though we have no idea how our questions stack up in terms of precise scientific measurement, we did find out how *bagels* stack up!

It seems that there are a few creative bagel eaters out there, but they are the exception. The basic observation is that most people haven't experimented all that much with bagels, mainly because they didn't know they could. Typical responses to our questions about bagel self-expression included:

"I never knew how to do it."

"I've never been given the opportunity to experiment."

"Lack of exposure."

"Didn't know you could."

"What I need is a cookbook to experiment with." (We loved that one!)

Some said it was difficult to get fresh bagels. We told them where to go—bagel-wise that is!

Among bagel purists, it was a different story. A strictly L & B (lox-and-bagel) type in New York replied, "I don't experiment because I'm old-fashioned and a traditionalist." Several other die-hards had similar replies or said, "I like it the way it is."

When did our respondents first start eating bagels? The answers ran the gamut from "in the crib," to "I only started two weeks ago" (this from a gentleman in his sixties). Teething on bagels as an infant was a popular response: approximately 16 percent of those surveyed said they had eaten bagels since infancy. "Since I had teeth." "In the crib." "For teething." "As soon as I had a tooth." One mother told us she gave her toddler a bagel on New Year's Eve so she and her husband could get some sleep after a night of celebrating!

Approximately 26 percent of those surveyed had their first bagel between age 3 and age 10. Another 22 percent had been introduced to bagels in their teens. Some 32 percent recalled eating their first bagels in their twenties, and an unfortunate 4 percent had reached age 30 before ever discovering the joy of bagel-eating.

Our survey found that people eat an average of 2.45 bagels per week, with respondents' replies ranging from a low of one-half to a high of 14 (this from an enthusiastic four-year-old who proclaimed that bagels are his favorite food in the whole world!).

Who Likes What?

These flavors, in order of preference, were our respondents choices:

FLAVOR	PERCENT	FLAVOR	PERCENT
plain	22.9	garlic	8.0
cinnamon-raisin	20.5	egg	2.0
onion	12.2	salt	2.0
sesame seed	12.2	wheat	2.0
poppyseed	8.2	rye	2.0
pumpernickel	8.0		

As we expected, most of the people questioned like their bagels with butter, cream cheese, or cream cheese spreads. (That's why we wrote this book!) Others like lox or nova and cream cheese. Or peanut butter.

The Bagels' "bagel originality" award for the most bizarre thing ever eaten on a bagel is a toss-up between the respondent who replied "squid," and the one who said "baked beans." Frankly, what others seemed to regard as strange we find normal:

"peanut butter and bacon"

"mozzarella cheese and tomato sauce"

"chicken salad"

"cream cheese, raisins and brown sugar spread"

"lunch meats"

"hummus"

"chocolate syrup and vanilla ice cream"

"egg omelet"

"shrimp salad"

Why Do You Like Bagels?

Here are some of the answers to our final question, which speak for themselves!

"Because they're crusty on the outside and soft on the inside."

"It's *the* unique flavor in all the world, and I like the way the cream cheese squishes up in the middle."

"Tastes soooo good!"

"You can eat them in bed and they don't make crumbs like crackers do."

"A nice change from bread and more filling."

"You can make a meal out of a bagel. It's substantial."

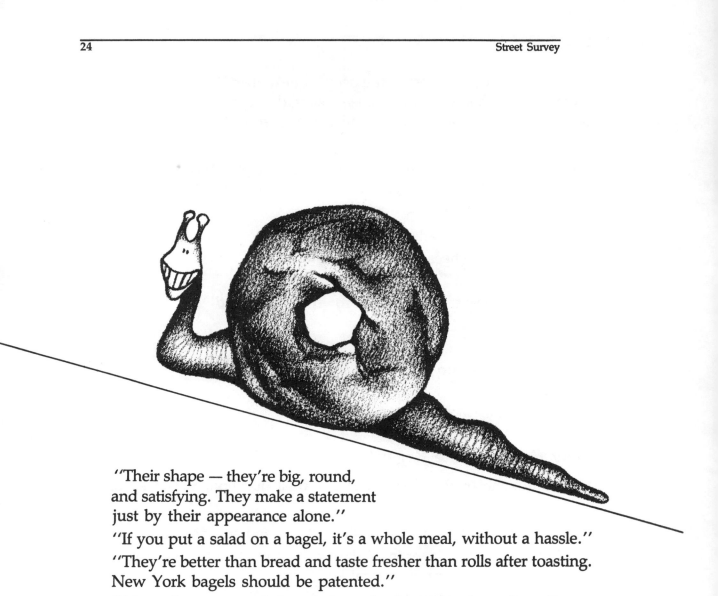

"Their shape — they're big, round,
and satisfying. They make a statement
just by their appearance alone."

"If you put a salad on a bagel, it's a whole meal, without a hassle."

"They're better than bread and taste fresher than rolls after toasting.
New York bagels should be patented."

"I love the taste, and they feel good when you chew them."

"Real bagels have a special texture unlike any other kind of bread.
They make *everything* taste better."

"They're perfect for business people. Three-bagel lunches should
replace three-martini lunches!"

Chapter 5

The Bagel Owner's Manual

Most people think bagels are just for breakfast. If you're one of these "bagel conservatives," think of all the fun you've been missing — bagels for snacks, bagels for lunch, bagels for dinner, and bagels for dessert! Well, you're about to come full-circle with us, because our bagel recipes will take you right through the day — from breakfast to bedtime. You'll have absolute confidence in each of our original, easy-to-follow recipes, which brought us countless compliments from our friends and taste-testers and will do the same for you. Want to plan a special evening with friends? Have a bagel party. Because everything's better with a bagel!

Incidentally, bagels freeze beautifully. If you buy your bagels already frozen from the grocer, simply store them in your freezer as is. When we buy bagels from a bagel bakery and they're still warm or hot, we find it best to let them cool in their paper bag before transferring them to plastic bags for storing or freezing. Otherwise they might get soggy. If you cut your bagels in half horizontally before freezing, you'll find them easier and more convenient to use straight from the freezer whenever the bagel mood strikes. Some people, by the way, think an old bagel is a dead bagel. Not so! Even if you have stale bagels, you can find many good uses for them, as you will discover in the chapters ahead. You can also freshen several-days-old bagels by putting them in a covered pot with a few drops of water and placing it in a 350° oven for 10 minutes or so.

You'll find that bagel halves are often too thick to fit into conventional toasters. Some manufacturers have, however, come out with toasters that have larger-than-standard-size openings, so you might want to be on the lookout for one of these. If you have a toaster oven, that's great. Or just heat them in a regular oven for about 5 minutes at 350°, or toast the halves under your broiler until they're just the way you like them.

You'll notice that many of our recipes call for using a foil-covered cookie sheet. That's because we're lazy and like to take the easy way out by not having to wash the cookie sheet. This way, you just toss out the aluminum foil when you've finished cooking.

One Word Of Bagel Caution; Bagels and microwaves really don't mix. We've found that bagels that are *heated* in our microwave come out very rubbery, unless you keep them in for just a couple of seconds. So our advice is to avoid heating them in this way. However, you CAN *defrost* frozen bagels successfully in the microwave for 50 seconds on the defrost setting, before toasting them in your toaster or oven. You can also use your microwave to restore stale bagels from the frozen state for approximately a minute and 10 seconds on the defrost setting.

Dieters will be delighted to know that you can add bagels to your menu — without adding guilt. One-half of a bagel has approximately the same number of calories as a slice of white bread and is lots more satisfying. What's more, bagels have no preservatives, contain no shortening and, except for egg bagels, have no cholesterol.

Certain bagel purists will tell you that the only way to enjoy bagels is with lots of fresh butter or cream cheese. That's pure baloney! (Which is, in fact, great on bagels, too.) Be imaginative as you enter the wonderful world of bageling. Our recipes are designed for both one and two-fisted eaters as well as for those who are strictly of the knife and fork persuasion. Just remember that the world is your bagel, and you can do with it what you wish. Here's to adventurous good eating!

Chapter 6

So You Want to Make Your Own Bagels?

First, take every recipe you have for making bagels and file them under "unbagels." That's what we had to do when we first tried to make our own bagels. All of the "expert" recipes we found in cookbooks and other publications produced sadly disappointing results—bagels that tasted more like pizza crust than bagels. We tried again and again, following instructions to the tiniest detail. You know what? We *still* got pizza dough!

When we had faced enough failures and found enough discrepancies among recipes to know what questions to ask professional bagel bakers, we did. Bread flour or all-purpose flour? Oil in the dough or no oil in the dough? A 375°, 425°, or 500° oven? Once-risen or twice-risen? Cake yeast or dry yeast? If you've tried to make your own bagels from recipes *you've* found from similar sources, you probably know what we're talking about. Not only do the recipes bear little resemblance to each other, they bear little resemblance to bagels.

But now that we've de-mystified the process for you, you can bake bagels to brag about.

Our recipe makes 16 delicious 3½-ounce bagels. By adding different toppings, you can create your own bakery assortment. We usually make 4 sesame seed, 4 poppy seed, 4 garlic, and 4 onion. It all starts with our basic water bagel recipe. If you prefer yours plain, simply eliminate the toppings.

We know you'll find bagel-making fun and be delighted with your results. Remember, though, that home-baked bagels do not exactly duplicate the texture that's achieved in a professional bagel bakery. In fact, so many variables can affect the outcome that maybe there out to be a Doctorate in Bagelology!

The-Recipe-That-Really-Works Bagels

What you need

2 0.6-ounce cakes of fresh yeast (We use Fleischmann's®
   fresh-active)

OR

2 $1/4$-ounce packets of active dry yeast. EITHER WORKS WELL.

$2^1/_2$ cups water

2 teaspoons sugar (ONLY IF YOU'RE USING DRY YEAST)

$2^1/_2$ teaspoons salt

$6^1/_8$ cups bread flour (should be high gluten—We use Pillsbury®
   Bread Flour "enriched bromated flour, naturally white, high
   protein, high gluten")

$1/_2$ cup corn meal

3 quarts water

   bottled sesame seeds, poppy seeds, dehydrated onion flakes,
   dehydrated minced garlic

2 cookie sheets and 2 pieces of burlap cut to fit each cookie sheet.
   (You can buy a roll of furniture burlap at any hardware store and
   keep it on hand for bagel baking.)

What you do

1. IF YOU USE CAKE YEAST: Be sure to note the expiration date
   printed on the package. If you have any doubt as to its freshness,
   crumble it; cake yeast is good if it crumbles readily. Dissolve cake
   yeast completely in $2^1/_2$ cups COOL WATER in a large mixing
   bowl. Let stand for 5 minutes. Then proceed to Step 2.

   IF YOU USE DRY YEAST: Place 2 packets of dry yeast in a glass
   with $1/_2$ cup WARM WATER (110°—the water will feel warm to

your fingertips) and stir in the 2 teaspoons of sugar. Mix until yeast is dissolved completely and set aside in a draft-free place for 5 minutes. The mixture should bubble up, producing a foamy layer on top. (If it doesn't bubble up, you probably used water that was too hot and killed the yeast, and you'll have to discard it and start again. If you have any doubts about the temperature, it's better to use water that's too cool.) Now pour the mixture into a large mixing bowl and add 2 cups of lukewarm water. You are now ready to proceed to Step 2.

2. Stir in salt.

3. Add $5^1/_2$ cups of flour, a cup at a time, mixing with a wooden spoon to blend after each addition. Dough will be sticky.

4. Spread $^1/_4$ cup of flour onto table or other kneading surface. Place dough on it. (You may have some dry flour remaining in the mixing bowl. Shake that onto the dough as well.) Then place an additional $^1/_4$ cup of flour on top of the dough.

5. Begin kneading slowly until flour comes together with rest of dough. Then knead vigorously for 10 minutes. You may find it necessary to add a bit of additional flour if the mixture is too sticky. That's what the extra $^1/_8$ cup flour is for. Use a bit at a time but no more than the $^1/_8$ cup. NOTE: Sometimes, depending on the weather—for instance, on a humid day—your dough may still be sticky and difficult to knead even after you add the $^1/_8$ cup of flour. At these times, simply dip your hands in flour, shake off the excess and continue kneading. You can do this as often as necessary. Just don't add additional amounts of flour to the dough. Your floured hands will be sufficient.

6. After kneading well for 10 minutes, use a sharp knife dipped in flour to cut the dough into 16 equal sections.

7. Now you have a choice as to how you want to form your bagels:

Option #1

Take each section of dough and roll it on a table or other flat surface till it is approximately 8 to $8^1/_2$ inches long. Then connect the ends by wrapping them around each other approximately 2 turns and tucking the ends underneath. Be sure to do this *securely* or the bagels will come apart during boiling. This is the method the professional bagel bakers use if they don't have bagel-making machines.

Option #2

This method is failure-proof because there is no risk of the bagels coming apart during boiling. Take each section of dough and roll it in your palms to make a ball. Flatten slightly, dip your index finger in flour and poke a hole through the center of the ball, working your finger around to make a hole a bit larger than the size of a quarter.

Either way you form your bagels, you'll have 16 when you finish.

8. Spread $\frac{1}{4}$ cup of corn meal on each of two wooden boards and place 8 formed bagels on each, leaving space in between the bagels. Cover with a towel and place in a draft-free spot for 45 minutes. (An UNHEATED oven is a perfect location.)

9. After 45 minutes, remove towel and place boards or trays of bagels uncovered in the refrigerator for 1 hour.

10. Meanwhile, preheat oven to 500°, with oven rack in the middle position.

11. In a large pot, bring 3 quarts of water to a boil.

12. Prepare your cookie sheets by wetting the pieces of burlap thoroughly, wringing them out, and placing them on each cookie sheet.

13. After you've refrigerated the bagels for an hour, remove them and place them, 4 at a time, in the boiling water. This stage is called "kettling." The perfect bagel, when kettled, should sink to the bottom of the pot of boiling water and rise immediately. Boil for 30 seconds on one side. Then, with a slotted spoon, turn the bagel onto the other side and kettle for 30 more seconds. If your bagels don't sink to the bottom when you first put them in the pot, don't worry. However, if they sink to the bottom and lay there, wait until they rise to the top (and they will) before timing your 30 seconds on each side.

14. After kettling, remove bagels with a slotted spoon and place on top of burlap-lined cookie sheets (8 on each). Then liberally sprinkle each with your choice of toppings. (It's fun to combine different toppings, too. One bagel baker we know makes an "E.T." bagel which stands for "everything on it.")

15. Now, place in a 500° oven for 3 minutes. This initial baking stage on burlap helps the bagel "skin" to form.

16. After 3 minutes, remove from oven and carefully slide the burlap and bagels off cookie sheets. Then, turn the bagels over and place them back onto the cookie sheets directly, *without* burlap.

17. Liberally sprinkle with toppings. Now your bagels have toppings on both sides, which makes them doubly good. Some people like to brush beaten egg on top before sprinkling toppings on. We find it makes it crustier than we like and don't recommend it.

18. Bake in the 500° oven for 20 minutes or until golden. Watch them carefully toward the end of your cooking time because everyone's oven is different. After taking them out of the oven, remove your bagels from the cookie sheets and let them cool for 10 minutes.

It will take all the willpower you have, but it's worth it. This recipe makes 16 wonderful bagels—made just the way you like them because you chose the toppings!

According to professional bagel bakers, it's difficult to make good bagels at home because of all the variables in the process. Making good bagels depends on many factors, each of which is significant: the proper quality high-gluten flour (professional bagel bakers use varieties of high-gluten flour that are not available in supermarkets), the quality of the water (hence the need for bakeries' water purification systems in some areas), the proper ratio of malt to flour, the right quantity of yeast, the right amount of salt (too much will affect the dough's ability to rise), the expertise of the doughmaker, the mixing, how the bagels are boiled, and so on. Every one of these things affects the outcome. On top of everything else, the weather conditions must be considered, because in a bagel bakery, the dough is prepared differently depending on what they are. As one bagel baker puts it, "Bagel dough is like a human being—it senses temperature." Thus, when the weather is warmer, professional bakers use less yeast. In humid or drier conditions, they make other adjustments.

The reason for refrigeration is that it retards the rising process and also affects the formation of the crust. Professionals actually refer to the refrigeration unit as a "retarder"; it has lower humidity than a standard refrigerator. Kettling—boiling the bagels—gives the bagels their special shine.

We found that more of the professionals we spoke with choose dry yeast over cake yeast. Some because it's easier to store. Others because it's just their preference. Some traditionalists, however swear by cake yeast. We also discovered the existence of "The Bagel Pipeline" when it comes to information. For instance, bagel bakers could tell us what brand of flour their competitors used and even when and if their competitors switched brands!

In a bagel bakery, the burlap stage is actually done on burlap-covered redwood boards. The burlap boards are wet down with water, after which the bagels are placed on them and put into the oven. Our burlap-covered cookie sheets take the place of these. Among bagel bakers, the expression "flipping the boards" describes the step of turning the bagels over from the burlap boards onto the oven hearth, which is how it's done in professional bakeries. Our recipe just calls for "flipping the bagels" back onto the cookie sheets!

It's gratifying and lots of fun to bake your own bagels at home, and fascinating to watch the professionals in action, too. Perhaps your neighborhood bagel bakers may be willing to take a moment when they're not too busy (although that's very hard to find!), and give you a behind-the-scenes peek.

Chapter 7

A. M. Bagels For Breakfast and Brunch

How good can a bagel brie?

The Big Cheese

What you need

2   bagels, cut in half horizontally
4 1/2 –ounce round of brie cheese, cut in thin slices
1/3   cup slivered almonds
   strawberry preserves

What you do

1. Cover each bagel half with slices of brie.
2. Top with slivered almonds and bake at 350° on foil-covered cookie sheet until cheese melts.
3. Serve with small spoonful of strawberry preserves. Makes 4 halves.

For hors d'oeuvres, cut each bagel half in sections, or use bagelettes.

These will click every time

Bagel Castanets

What you need

1 bagel, cut in half horizontally, toasted and buttered

2 eggs

2 tablespoons water

2 tablespoons margarine or butter

2 tablespoons finely chopped onion or scallions (spring onions)

2 tablespoons finely diced green pepper

1 tablespoon finely chopped black olives

2 tablespoons chopped fresh tomatoes

1 ounce diced pastrami or corned beef
    freshly ground pepper to taste
    bottled mild taco sauce, warmed

What you do

1. In bowl, beat eggs and add water and freshly ground pepper.

2. Add chopped onion, green pepper, olives, tomato, and choice of meat. Mix well.

3. Melt margarine or butter in frypan over medium heat; add egg mixture and scramble until done.

4. Spoon half the mixture onto each buttered, toasted bagel half; top with taco sauce. Makes 2 halves.

Refrigerate what's left (if there is any!) to enjoy later.

Bagelberries

What you need
bagels, cut in half, toasted and buttered
1 cup ricotta cheese (regular or low-fat part skim)
   10-ounce package frozen raspberries, thawed and drained
1 cup blueberries (if you can't get fresh, use frozen, thawed and drained)
1 tablespoon powdered sugar (or artificial sweetener)

What you do
1. In small bowl, blend ricotta cheese, raspberries, blueberries and sugar.
2. Cut toasted, buttered bagel halves in sections and dunk your way through breakfast. Makes about $1\frac{1}{2}$ cups.

Nothing fishy about

For-Herring-Lovers-Only Bagels

What you need
bagels, cut in half horizontally
1 8-ounce jar of herring in cream sauce

What you do
Spoon herring in cream sauce onto toasted bagel halves.

Have the brunch bunch over for...

Bagels Benedict

What you need
2 bagels, cut in half horizontally
   margarine or butter
4 slices balogna
4 poached eggs
   Hollandaise Sauce*
   fresh parsley sprigs to garnish

What you do
1. Toast and butter bagel halves.
2. Heat slices of balogna in frypan and place a slice on each bagel half.
3. Top each with poached egg; pour on Hollandaise. Makes 4 halves.

*To make blender Hollandaise, heat ½ cup butter or margarine until melted and hot. Don't let it brown. Meanwhile, put 3 egg yolks, 1 tablespoon lemon juice and a dash each of white pepper and salt in a blender and blend well. Pour in hot butter or margarine, and blend for a second or two. Makes ¾ cup sauce.

Keep this on hand in the refrigerator so it's ready when you are.

<u>*Great on bagelettes, too!*</u>

A Honey-Of-a-Bagel Spread

What you need
    bagels, cut in half horizontally
1½ tablespoons honey
 ½ cup soft margarine or butter
 2 tablespoons golden raisins

What you do
1. Mix honey and margarine or butter together.
2. Add raisins and mix again.
3. Spread on toasted bagels, Makes about ½ cup of bagel spread.

<u>*Norman wouldn't steer you wrong!*</u>

Norman's Favorite Bagel

What you need
1 bagel, cut in half horizontally
4 ounces smoked whitefish or 2 slices sable fish (from your favorite deli)
4 slices of cucumber
  mayonnaise

What you do
1. With fingers, scoop out insides of bagel halves (freeze for other use)
2. Place whitefish or sable on bottom half. Top with cucumber slices.
3. Spread mayonnaise on other bagel half and place on top. Serves 1.

We're not kidding! They're delicious, and a great way to use up stale bagels.

Bagel Pancakes

What you need

3 bagels
3 eggs, beaten
1½ cups milk
¼ plus ⅛ teaspoon salt
¾ teaspoon sugar
½ teaspoon vanilla
margarine or butter for frying

What you do

1. Cut bagels in small chunks and put in blender or food processor a few at a time, grinding into crumbs.
2. Place crumbs in mixing bowl and add beaten eggs, milk, salt, sugar, and vanilla. Mix very well. Mixture will be thick.
3. Heat margarine or butter in griddle or large frypan.
4. With large spoon or heaping tablespoon, spoon batter into pan (as you would regular pancakes). Flatten each with back of spoon.
5. Cook slowly over medium heat. You may want to add additional margarine or butter as they cook to keep pan from becoming dry. Cook each side until golden brown.
6. Serve with syrup, preserves, honey, or powdered sugar. Makes 12 bagel pancakes. (If you want to make less, one bagel makes 4 bagel pancakes. Reduce other ingredients accordingly.)

For a delightful variation, add grated apple to the batter before frying. Remember, you can freeze leftover pancakes, and reheat in oven (or microwave, if you're in a rush).

Colorado combination with a new twist

Denver Bagels

What you need

1 bagel, sliced in half horizontally, heated or toasted and buttered
2 eggs, beaten with 2 tablespoons water
4 ounces pastrami or bologna, diced
1 tablespoon finely chopped green pepper
1 tablespoon finely chopped onion
1 tablespoon butter or margarine
   dash of pepper
   dash of oregano

What you do

1. Mix your choice of meat with green pepper, onion, pepper, and oregano.
2. Add beaten egg mixture and blend well.
3. Heat margarine or butter in frypan and scramble until firm.
4. Divide mixture and place on buttered bagel halves. Serve open-faced. Makes 2 halves.

William will never Tell...

Apple-Peanut Butter Bagels

What you need

 2 bagels, cut in half horizontally
   soft margarine or butter
1/3 cup creamy peanut butter
1/8 cup plus 1 tablespoon applesauce
1/8 cup finely chopped unpeeled red apple

What you do

1. Lightly spread bagels with margarine or butter.

2 . Place peanut butter and applesauce in small bowl. Mix until smooth.

3 . Stir in chopped apple. Blend well.

4 . Spread onto bagel halves. Makes 4 halves.

Breakfast bonanza

Scrambled Bagel

What you need

1 bagel

1 egg

2 tablespoons cream cheese, cut in small pieces

1 tablespoon milk

freshly ground pepper

salt to taste

1 teaspoon butter or margarine

chopped scallions (spring onions) or chives, if desired

What you do

1. Slice off top quarter of bagel horizontally.

2 . Carefully scoop out inside of bagel with your fingers and set aside bagel bits, leaving a bagel "shell."

3 . Heat bagel shell and top in oven; while they are warming, beat egg with fork or whisk.

4 . Finely crumble the bagel bits you scooped out; add crumbs to egg.

5 . Add cream cheese, milk, salt, and pepper, and scallions if desired.

6 . Melt butter or margarine in a frypan and scramble egg until dry set.

7 . Fill warmed bagel shell with cooked egg and replace bagel top. Serves 1.

For variety, experiment with shredded cheeese or sliced mushrooms added to the egg mixture before cooking.

This one's right on target. (Especially good with garlic or onion bagels.)

Bullseye Bagels

What you need
1 bagel, cut in half horizontally
2 eggs
2 slices bologna
2 teaspoons margarine or butter
   freshly ground pepper

What you do
1. Toast bagel halves lightly in toaster or oven
   and butter with ½ teaspoon on each.
2. Meanwhile, heat bologna slices on both sides in frypan and place
   atop each toasted and buttered bagel half.
3. In frypan, add remaining teaspoon butter or margarine and fry the
   eggs until whites are set.
4. Sprinkle with freshly ground pepper and put each egg on top of
   bologna slice. Serve open-faced. Makes 2 halves.

This old standby's not just for lunch. Try it for breakfast—on a bagel, of course.

P & J Bagels

What you need
1 bagel, cut in half horizontally
   peanut butter, smooth or crunchy
   your favorite jelly or preserves

What you do
1. Toast bagel halves in toaster or oven.
2. While still hot, spread with peanut butter (it gets melty and
   delicious) and top with jelly or preserves. Makes 2 halves or 1
   bagel sandwich.

A refreshing light breakfast

Strawberries 'n' Cream Bagels

What you need

  1 bagel, sliced in half horizontally

  1 teaspoon margarine or butter

$\frac{1}{2}$ cup ricotta cheese (regular or low-fat part skim)

$\frac{3}{4}$ cup fresh strawberries

$\frac{1}{2}$ teaspoon granulated sugar (or artificial sweetener)

     fresh mint (if available)

What you do

1. Toast bagel in toaster or oven and lightly butter.
2. Mash $\frac{1}{4}$ cup strawberries and mix with ricotta cheese and sugar.
3. Blend well and spread each bagel half with mixture.
4. Slice remaining half-cup of strawberries and place on top of ricotta cheese.
5. Garnish with mint leaves, if desired. Serve open-faced. Makes 2 halves.

Raisin' your bagel-consciousness

Raisin In The Bun

What you need

  1 cinnamon-raisin bagel, cut in half horizontally

$\frac{1}{2}$ cup cottage cheese, mashed with a fork

  1 tablespoon golden raisins

  1 teaspoon brown sugar (or artificial sweetener)

What you do

1. Blend cottage cheese and brown sugar together

2. Add raisins and mix well.
3. Spread on bottom half of bagel and add top half. (You may want to heat the bagel before you spoon on the mixture.) Serves 1.

Try ricotta cheese (regular or low-fat part skim) instead of cottage cheese for an exotic taste.

Your French-toast days will never be the same!

Irma La Bagel

What you need
  1 bagel, sliced in half horizontally
  1 egg
  1 tablespoon milk
  ¼ teaspoon vanilla
     dash of cinnamon
     dash of salt
  ¼ teaspoon sugar
  2 teaspoons margarine or butter
     powdered sugar

What you do
1. Mix together egg, milk, vanilla, cinnamon, salt, and sugar. Beat with fork.
2. Pierce tops of bagel halves and place in egg mixture cut-side down. Soak for about 5 minutes; turn to coat both sides.
3. Melt 2 teaspoons margarine in frypan and add bagel halves. Cook slowly over medium heat until brown on both sides and cooked through. (The cut sides will need extra cooking time.)
4. Sprinkle with powdered sugar and serve open-faced. Or top with blueberry or strawberry preserves, syrup, or honey. Makes 2 halves.

For "salmon"- chanted morning

The Traditional Bagel

What you need
1 bagel, cut in half horizontally

2 good-sized slices smoked salmon ("Nova" has a more delicate flavor, "lox" is stronger and saltier)

cream cheese

2 thick tomato slices

2 thin onion slices, optional

What you do
1. Spread bagel halves with cream cheese.
2. Top each with slice of smoked salmon, tomato slice, and onion, if desired.
3. Serve open-faced, or diners with big mouths can make a sandwich. Makes 2 halves or 1 bagel sandwich.

Kids of all ages, including adult types, will enjoy these!

Circus Bagels

What you need
1 bagel, cut in half horizontally

4 tablespoons crunchy peanut butter

$\frac{1}{2}$ banana, sliced

2 teaspoons coconut

What you do
1. Spread toasted or plain bagel halves with crunchy peanut butter.
2. Top with banana slices and sprinkle with coconut. Makes 2 halves.

Chapter 8

Bagel Bits and Bites
from Snacks to Hearty Meals

¡Muy delicioso!

Bagelitos (Bagel Nachos)

What you need
bagel chips (You can buy them by the bag.)
15-ounce can chili without beans
4-ounce package shredded cheddar cheese
4-ounce can mild chopped green chilies

What you do
1. On each bagel chip place a heaping teaspoon chili; top with a teaspoon of cheddar cheese and $1/2$ teaspoon chilies. If you have bagel chip pieces instead of whole chips, adjust quantities accordingly.
2. Bake on aluminum-foil-covered cookie sheet in 375° oven until cheese melts. (This is *one* recipe you can do in the microwave, on a microwave platter for 50 seconds on high setting, or until cheese melts. You may need a bit more time if you're cooking a platter-full.) Makes 15, if you use unbroken bagel chips.

These are really great munchies! Assemble them for cooking just before company comes or they might get soggy.

You won't have the strength to resist these!

Health Bagels

What you need
   1 bagel, cut in half horizontally
      mayonnaise
   1 small avocado, peeled and sliced
   2 tablespoons alfalfa sprouts
$\frac{1}{2}$ cup shredded Monterey Jack cheese
   2 tablespoons sesame chips, crumbled

What you do
1. Spread bagel halves with mayonnaise.
2. Place avocado slices,
   then alfalfa sprouts on each half.
3. Put $\frac{1}{4}$ cup of cheese on each and top with
   sesame chips. Makes 2 halves.

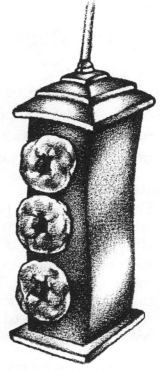

An easy hors d'oeuvre that tastes like white pizza!

Bagels Italiano

What you need
bagels, cut in half horizontally
margarine
bottled Italian salad dressing
grated parmesan cheese
oregano
dash of garlic powder

What you do
1. Spread bagel halves with margarine and place on foil-covered cookie sheet. Cut each half in 4 sections.
2. Carefully spoon 1 teaspoon of Italian dressing on top of each section.
3. Sprinkle with parmesan cheese, oregano, and garlic powder.
4. Place cookie sheet in a 375° oven and bake for 10 minutes.

Bet these will light your fire.

Bagel-Ques

What you need
2 bagels, cut in half horizontally
1 pound ground beef
1/4 teaspoon garlic powder

1 onion, finely chopped

1 tablespoon brown sugar

$^1/_2$ cup barbecue sauce (any kind)

What you do

1. With fingers, scoop out insides of bagel halves, leaving ''shells,'' and put bagel bits in blender, making fine crumbs.
2. In frypan over medium heat, crumble ground beef, add garlic powder and chopped onion, and cook thoroughly. Drain off fat.
3. Add brown sugar, bagel crumbs, and barbecue sauce and stir well over low heat.
4. Fill bagel shells with meat mixture and bake on foil-covered cookie sheet in 375° oven for about 15 minutes or until heated thoroughly. Makes 4 halves.

New accent on an old favorite

Rumaki Bagels

What you need

3 bagels, cut in half horizontally

1 pound chicken livers, drained

   8-ounce can water chestnuts, drained and chopped

2 tablespoons bottled teriyaki sauce

1 teaspoon sugar

$^1/_4$ cup mayonnaise

   fresh parsley to garnish

What you do

1. In frypan, cook chicken livers with 1 tablespoon teriyaki sauce. As chicken livers cook, cut them into small pieces with knife and fork.

2. When chicken livers are completely cooked, remove pan from heat and add 1 tablespoon teriyaki sauce and sugar, water chestnuts. Mix thoroughly.

3. Add mayonnaise to the mixture and blend well.

4. Spoon onto bagel halves. Garnish with fresh parsley and refrigerate until serving time. You can also serve these warm. Just heat in a 375° oven. Makes 6 halves.

This recipe freezes beautifully.

A deli-cious discovery

Deli Boss Bagel

What you need

 1 bagel, cut in half horizontally
    mustard
 3 ounces pastrami
 1 slice swiss cheese
$1/4$ cup coleslaw (or a bit less)

What you do

1. Spread bagel halves with thin coat of mustard.
2. On one bagel half, place pastrami and swiss cheese.
3. Top with coleslaw and other bagel half. Serves 1.

It rises to the occasion!

Bagel Souffle

What you need
 4 bagels, cut in half horizontally

$1/4$ cup plus 1 tablespoon margarine or butter

 6 ounces Monterey Jack cheese, grated

 6 ounces cheddar cheese, grated

 7 eggs

$1/2$ teaspoon salt

 2 cups milk

$1/4$ teaspoon paprika

  freshly ground pepper

What you do
1. Grease a 2-quart casserole with 2 tablespoons of margarine or butter.
2. Butter each bagel half with approximately 1 teaspoon margarine or butter; cut bagel halves into small bite-size pieces and set aside.
3. In a mixing bowl beat together eggs, salt, milk, paprika, and pepper.
4. Place half the bagel cubes in greased casserole. Mix cheeses together and place half of cheese mixture on top of bagel cubes; repeat with rest of bagel cubes and rest of cheese.
5. Carefully ladle egg mixture into casserole dish on top of bagel-cheese layers making sure to cover evenly so it seeps through. (You may want to poke holes through with a knife as you ladle.)
6. Set casserole in refrigerator and let stand overnight, and until you are ready to bake it the next day.
7. Bake casserole in a 350° oven for 1 hour.

Absolutely scrumptious! Every bite is heavenly!

Like nothing you've ever tasted. You'll want seconds!

Bagel Slaw

What you need

  1 bagel, cut in small bite-size cubes

  2 cups shredded cabbage

  6 ounces bologna, cut in half and then into thin strips

  4 ounces Monterey Jack cheese, shredded

  1 carrot, peeled and grated

$1/4$ cup plus 1 tablespoon mayonnaise or salad dressing
    freshly ground pepper

What you do

1. In a mixing bowl, combine shredded cabbage, bologna strips, grated cheese, and grated carrot.
2. Add mayonnaise or salad dressing and pepper and mix well. You can make ahead to this point.
3. Just before serving, add bagel cubes and mix thoroughly. Serves 4.

Do you have a favorite stew recipe? Serve it over open-faced bagels for a new treat!

Bagels Bourguignonne

What you need
   bagels, cut in half horizontally
2 pounds pot roast cut in cubes, or use stew beef chunks
1 cup flour
1 teaspoon seasoned salt
   cooking oil for browning
1 cup beef consomme
½ cup dry white wine
1 garlic clove, minced
1 onion, finely chopped
2 carrots, peeled and julienned
2 stalks celery, finely chopped

What you do
1. Mix flour and seasoned salt together and put in plastic bag. Add beef cubes and toss thoroughly to coat with flour mixture.
2. Place cooking oil in large heavy saucepan and brown beef thoroughly.
3. Pour beef consomme and wine over beef.
4. Add minced garlic, chopped onion, carrots, and celery and stir well.
5. Bring to a boil; reduce heat and let simmer for 2 to 3 hours, stirring periodically.
6. Serve over hot bagel halves. Serves 4.

Don't let this one get away.

Fish & Chips

What you need
   bagel chips
$\frac{1}{2}$ pound fish fillet, any kind, cooked
$\frac{1}{4}$ cup mayonnaise or salad dressing
 1 stalk celery, chopped fine
$\frac{1}{2}$ teaspoon Old Bay® Seasoning
 1 teaspoon dehydrated onion flakes
   ground pepper to taste

What you do
1. Crumble fish in mixing bowl with fork.
2. Add mayonnaise or salad dressing and mix well.
3. Add chopped celery, Old Bay® seasoning, onion flakes, and pepper and mix until well blended. Serve as a dip with bagel chips.

This is also good spooned on bagel halves, or atop shredded lettuce with a toasted bagel on the side.

Move over, McD's!

Bagel Burger

What you need
 1 bagel, sliced in half horizontally
$\frac{1}{4}$ lb. hamburger patty
$\frac{1}{4}$ onion, chopped or sliced
   shredded lettuce
   bottled thousand island salad dressing

What you do

1. You can heat or toast the bagel, or use it plain.
2. Fry hamburger patty in onions and place on bottom half of bagel.
3. Top with shredded lettuce, thousand island salad dressing, and other bagel half. Then get ready to open wide! Serves 1.

Who wants to peel potatoes?

Bagels 'n' Gravy

What you need
bagels, cut in half horizontally
leftover gravy from roast or
12-ounce jar of bottled "homestyle" gravy

What you do
1. Heat gravy in saucepan.
2. Spoon over heated or toasted bagel halves.

Choose whatever flavor bottled gravy you prefer, or make your own. Brown gravy, chicken gravy, mushroom gravy, turkey gravy, and onion gravy are all great on bagels!

Party-time favorites

Cheesey Bagel Chips

What you need
bagel chips (you can buy them by the bag)
10-ounce can Frito-Lay's® brand Milk Cheddar or Zesty Cheddar & Herb Cheese Dip
bottled bacon bits

What you do
1. Heat bagel chips in oven till warm.
2. Meanwhile, heat cheese dip in small saucepan, stirring as it heats.
3. Place warmed bagel chips on serving plate.
4. Spoon warmed cheese dip over chips.
5. Sprinkle with bacon bits and serve.

Let's play...

Ring Around The Bagel

What you need

2 onion bagels, cut in half horizontally

$1/2$ cup cream cheese

2 hard boiled eggs, chopped fine

1 small onion, chopped fine

$1/2$ cup canned tuna or canned salmon

What you do

1. Spread each bagel half with approximately $1/8$ cup of cream cheese, spreading completely to the edges and covering bagel hole.

2. Use a small spoon to carefully place chopped egg onto cream cheese to form a circle at the outside edge of the bagel halves. Press egg gently into cream cheese. When you've finished, each one will look like a ''wreath '' of chopped egg.

3. Make a circle of chopped onion inside the circle of chopped egg.

4. Spoon tuna or salmon into center circle of each bagel half. Makes 4 halves.

This is a very versatile recipe. If you don't care for caviar, you can try tuna-onion-egg, or chives-onion-canned salmon combinations. They're all delectable.

And for you Texans...

Chicken Fried Bagels

What you need

2 bagels cut in half horizontally
1 tablespoon cooking oil
1 egg, beaten
$\frac{1}{2}$ cup plus 1 tablespoon milk
1 teaspoon baking powder
$\frac{1}{4}$ teaspoon salt
$\frac{1}{8}$ teaspoon pepper
$\frac{1}{4}$ teaspoon paprika
$\frac{1}{4}$ teaspoon garlic powder
1 cup flour
   oil for frying
   honey

What you do

1. In mixing bowl, beat oil and egg with fork.
2. Add milk, baking powder, salt, pepper, paprika, and garlic powder. Beat thoroughly with egg beater.
3. Add flour and beat until well mixed. Batter will be thick.
4. Place bagel halves in batter one at a time, and using spoon and fork, coat with batter on both sides.
5. In large frypan, heat about 1 inch of cooking oil. Over medium heat, fry bagels on cut side first, then when golden brown, turn with fork and cook on other side until golden brown.
6. Drain on paper towels. Serve warm with a side dish of honey for dipping. Makes 4 halves.

If you prefer, you can dip these in a white sauce gravy instead of honey.

Charlie never had it so good.

Bagel Tuna Boats

What you need

    4 bagels

$6\frac{1}{2}$-ounce can of white tuna packed in water, drained

$10\frac{1}{2}$-ounce can cream of mushroom soup

    2 tablespoons fresh parsley, chopped

    $\frac{1}{2}$ of an 8-ounce can of water chestnuts, drained and chopped

    2 tablespoons margarine or butter

What you do

1. With serrated knife, slice a thin portion off the top of each bagel and with the fingers, scoop out insides of bagels and reserve, leaving bagel "boats." Set aside.
2. Put drained tuna in mixing bowl and separate into fine pieces with fingers.
3. Fold in undiluted can of cream of mushroom soup, water chestnuts, and parsley, and mix until well blended.
4. Fill each bagel boat with a little less than a half-cup of tuna mixture.
5. Crumble some of the scooped-out bagel bits with your fingers (or in blender or food processor) to make fine crumbs.
6. In frypan melt margarine or butter and add the crumbs, stirring quickly until light brown.
7. Sprinkle crumbs on top of tuna mixture in bagels and bake on foil-covered cookie sheet in 375° oven for about 15 to 20 minutes or until thoroughly heated. Makes 4 (You can put bagel tops and some of the bagel bits you didn't use for crumbs into a plastic bag and freeze for later use. You can also freeze the filled boats and just reheat in oven.)

When in Rome...

Pizza Bagels

What you need

 1 bagel, cut in half horizontally

$1/2$ cup shredded mozzarella cheese

$1/4$ cup chunk-style spaghetti sauce or pizza sauce

 1 small can sliced mushrooms, drained

 2 dashes oregano

What you do

1. Put $1/8$ cup spaghetti sauce or pizza sauce on each bagel half.
2. Sprinkle dash of oregano on sauce and top each with mushroom slices and $1/4$ cup of mozzarella cheese.
3. Bake on foil-covered cookie sheet in 375° oven for 8-10 minutes, or until cheese bubbles and begins to brown. Makes 2 halves.

You can use any of your favorite pizza toppings. Try sliced olives, cooked mushrooms, sauteed green pepper and onion, and anchovies.

Irresistible on a cold winter's evening!

Soup 'n' Bagels

What you need

For a fun meal, make a tureen-full of your favorite hearty soup. Serve with a big basket of assorted hot, toasty buttered bagels.

Here's a rare one...

Bagel Tartare

What you need
3 bagels, sliced in half horizontally
$^3/_4$ pound ground sirloin
$^1/_2$ teaspoon salt
$^1/_2$ teaspoon garlic powder
   ground pepper to taste
$^1/_2$ cup finely chopped green pepper
$^1/_2$ cup finely chopped onions
$^1/_4$ cup chopped fresh parsley
1 tablespoon capers, optional

What you do
1. Mix ground sirloin, salt, garlic powder, pepper, green pepper, onions, and capers. Blend very well.
2. Spread on bagel halves and sprinkle with chopped parsley to garnish. Makes 6 halves. Excellent on onion or garlic bagels.

Don't make this too far ahead because meat may discolor.

Please pass the cheese crowd-pleasers.

Bleu Bagels

What you need
2 bagels, sliced in half horizontally
$^1/_2$ cup mayonnaise
1 cup crumbled bleu cheese
4 tomato slices
1 tablespoon dried or fresh chopped parsley

What you do
1. Mix mayonnaise, parsley, and bleu cheese together.
2. Spread onto bagel halves.
3. Place under broiler until cheese has melted.
4. Remove and top each with tomato slice. Makes 4 halves.

<u>*Another great use for stale bagels!*</u>

Bagel Stuffing

What you need
3 bagels, cut into small cubes
1 stalk celery, chopped
$1/2$ cup margarine
1 medium onion, chopped
8 mushrooms, chopped
$1/8$ cup chopped fresh parsley
$1/4$ teaspoon poultry seasoning
2 eggs, beaten

What you do
1. Put bagel cubes on foil-covered cookie sheet and bake in 375° oven for 15 minutes. Place in mixing bowl.
2. In large frypan, melt margarine and saute celery, onion, mushrooms, and parsley until vegetables are tender.
3. Stir in poultry seasoning and mix thoroughly.
4. Pour mixture over bagel cubes in bowl and mix well.
5. Add 2 beaten eggs and mix thoroughly. Refrigerate stuffing mixture until cold before stuffing poultry.

This recipe makes enough to stuff 8 pounds of poultry. Cut recipe in half to stuff a 4-pound chicken.

A scrumptious combination! You'll make these again and again.

Alice Bagel's Bagels

What you need

 4 bagels, cut in half horizontally

 3 tablespoons soft margarine or butter

 3 tablespoons mustard

 1 pound very lean ground beef

 $\frac{1}{4}$ cup catsup

 1 onion (small or medium) chopped fine

 $\frac{1}{4}$ teaspoon garlic powder

 $\frac{1}{4}$ teaspoon seasoned salt

What you do

1. Place bagel halves under the broiler until cut side is toasted.

2. Meanwhile, blend soft margarine or butter together with mustard.

3. Remove bagel halves from oven and spread completely to the edges with margarine-mustard mixture. (You'll use half of the mixture for this, the rest at the end of the recipe.)

4. In a bowl, place ground beef, catsup, chopped onion, garlic powder, and seasoned salt, and mix well with hands.

5. Divide mixture into four portions. Take one portion of meat, divide it in half again and press each onto each half of bagel completely to the edges.

6. Repeat with rest of bagels.

7. Place all under broiler for about 10 to 12 minutes or until meat is cooked.

8. Remove from oven and immediately spread the top of each with remaining margarine-mustard mixture. Makes 8 halves.

It's like bringing a New York deli into your kitchen!

Whopper Bagel

What you need
1 bagel, cut in half horizontally
4 ounces corned beef (heated or cold)
¼ cup coleslaw
1 teaspoon catsup
1 tablespoon mayonnaise

What you do
1. Place corned beef on bottom bagel half and top with coleslaw.
2. Mix catsup and mayonnaise together; spread on other bagel half and place on top. This recipe makes one whopper of a bagel! Serves 1. (If you prefer, serve it open-faced on 2 halves.)

These are right on the money for parties or TV munchies.

Bagel Coins

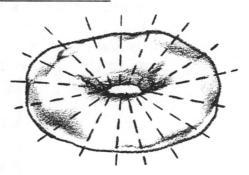

What you need
3 bagels, sliced in thin "coins" as shown, using serrated knife
1 cup cooking oil
1 garlic clove, minced
(use a garlic press, if you have one)
¼ cup grated parmesan cheese
   dry-roasted peanuts

What you do
1. Put cup of cooking oil in large frypan, add minced garlic and stir well. (For onion-flavored coins, use dehydrated onion flakes in oil instead of garlic clove.)
2. Heat oil and add bagel "coins." Fry until brown and crisp on both sides.

3. Drain on paper towels. When cool, place in plastic bag and toss well with parmesan cheese.

4. Remove from bag, mix with peanuts, and serve.

They store well in a tightly capped jar.

Pressed for a tempting sandwich? Try —

The Iron Bagel

What you need
1 bagel, sliced horizontally
2 teaspoons mayonnaise or salad dressing
½ cup chopped liver
1 slice tomato

What you do
1. Spread each bagel half with a teaspoon of mayonnaise or salad dressing.
2. Top with chopped liver and tomato slices and make a bagel sandwich. Serves 1.

If your bagel bakery makes cheese-flavored bagels, try them with this tasty topping.

Easy-Cheesey Bagels

What you need

1 bagel, sliced in half horizontally
2 tablespoons cream cheese
2 ounces cheddar cheese, shredded
2 ounces Monterey Jack cheese, shredded
4 stuffed green olives, sliced

What you do

1. Spread each bagel half with a tablespoon of cream cheese.
2. Mix cheddar and Monterey Jack cheeses together and spoon onto halves. Top with olive slices. Makes 2 halves.

Say "ole" three times before eating...

Mexicali Bagel Fondue

What you need

3 bagels, cut in half horizontally
4 tablespoons margarine
1 small onion, finely chopped
   4-ounce can mild chopped green chilies
   flour
1 15-ounce can tomatoes, mashed
   worcestershire sauce to taste
   garlic powder to taste
12 ounces shredded cheddar cheese

What you do

1. Toast bagel halves in toaster or oven.
2. Cut each half into tenths, vertically, and set aside.

3. In frypan brown onion in margarine and add chilies.
4. Add enough flour to make a thick paste.
5. Add tomatoes, and lots of worcestershire sauce and garlic powder, and mix well.
6. Stir in shredded cheddar cheese and blend all together over heat.
7. Serve in fondue pot with toasted bagel chunks.

This topping has an Italian accent!

Bagels Parmesan

What you need
 2 bagels, cut in half horizontally
 1 cup grated parmesan cheese
$\frac{1}{2}$ cup mayonnaise
 1 medium onion, grated
    dash of paprika

What you do
1. Mix cheese with mayonnaise and onion, and blend well.
2. Spread onto bagel halves; sprinkle with a dash of paprika.
3. Bake in 375° oven for 10 minutes. Makes 4 halves.

Fragrant and tempting

Bagel Garlic Bread

What you need
4 bagels, cut in half horizontally
8 teaspoons soft margarine, or butter, or more if desired
    garlic powder
    oregano
    grated parmesan cheese

What you do

1. Spread each bagel half with 1 teaspoon margarine or butter. Use more if desired.
2. Generously sprinkle with garlic powder, oregano, and parmesan cheese.
3. Cut each half in half again vertically.
4. Place on foil-covered cookie sheet in 375° oven and bake until thoroughly heated and tops start to brown. Makes 16 pieces.

You'll love this one—fer sure!

California Bagel Spread

What you need

bagels, cut in half horizontally
4-ounce package of cream cheese, softened
$\frac{1}{8}$ cup golden raisins
$1\frac{1}{2}$ tablespoons honey
1 medium carrot, peeled and grated
$\frac{1}{4}$ cup chopped walnuts

What you do

1. Mix cream cheese and honey together.
2. Add raisins, grated carrot, and walnuts.
3. Spread on bagels. Makes approximately 1 cup of spread.

Especially great with garlic or onion bagel

Poor Boy Bagel

What you need
1 bagel, sliced in half horizontally
2 thick slices of salami or bologna
1 lettuce leaf
2 teaspoons mayonnaise or salad dressing
2 thin slices tomato

What you do
1. Spread bagel halves with mayonnaise or salad dressing.
2. Place salami slices on bottom half, top with lettuce leaf, tomato slices, and other bagel half. Serves 1.

Mediterranean flavors combine in the...

Kojak Bagel

What you need
1 bagel, sliced in half horizontally
   olive oil
   shredded lettuce
4 ounces feta cheese, crumbled
2 slices tomato
2 thin slices onion
4 greek olives, sliced (or anchovies, if you prefer)

What you do
1. Sprinkle bagel halves very lightly with olive oil.
2. Place small amount of shredded lettuce on each.
3. Add feta cheese, onion, and tomato slices; top with sliced olives. Makes 2 halves.

These will melt in your mouth!

Bagel Melts

What you need

2 bagels, cut in half horizontally

7$\frac{1}{2}$-ounce can white tuna packed in water, well drained and flaked

$\frac{1}{4}$ cup mayonnaise

1 tomato, cut into cubes

1 stalk celery, chopped

4 slices cheddar cheese

What you do

1. Mix tuna, mayonnaise, tomato cubes, and celery until well blended. Spoon onto bagel halves.
2. Top each with slice of cheddar cheese.
3. Place under broiler and cook until cheese melts. Makes 4 halves.

You won't be sari you tried this one.

Delhi Bagels

What you need

1 bagel, cut in half horizontally

$\frac{1}{2}$ cup soft or whipped cream cheese

$\frac{1}{4}$ teaspoon plus $\frac{1}{8}$ teaspoon curry powder

2 teaspoons chutney

$\frac{1}{8}$ cup finely chopped unsalted peanuts

1 tablespoon coconut

What you do

1. Mix cream cheese, curry powder, chutney, peanuts and coconut, and blend well.
2. Spread on bagel halves. Makes 2 halves.

If you like curry, you'll love this. Try it on bagelettes, too.

Gather the group for

Bagel Beer Fondue

What you need
5 bagels, cut in large bite-size chunks
1 small garlic clove, halved
$3/4$ cup beer
8 ounces swiss cheese, shredded
4 ounces sharp cheddar cheese, shredded
1 tablespoon flour
   freshly ground pepper
$1/8$ teaspoon paprika

What you do
1. Rub the inside of a heavy saucepan with garlic; discard garlic.
2. Add beer and heat slowly.
3. Place flour in a plastic bag, add shredded cheeses, and shake to coat.
4. Gradually add cheese mixture to beer. Stir constantly until thickened and bubbly, but do not boil.
5. Stir in pepper and paprika.
6. Pour into fondue pot and serve with bagel chunks. Spear chunks and dip into hot cheese mixture to coat. (Add more warmed beer if fondue becomes too thick.)

Have your bagels lost their freshness? Turn 'em into croutons! A terrific way to top off any salad bowl.

Bagel Croutons

What you need
3 bagels, cut into cubes
1 cup cooking oil

1 garlic clove, thinly sliced

$\frac{1}{2}$ cup grated parmesan cheese
dried or chopped fresh parsley

What you do

1. Place 1 cup cooking oil in a small bowl with garlic for 1 hour; discard garlic.
2. Heat garlic oil in large frypan, add bagel cubes and cook till crispy golden brown, tossing constantly.
3. Drain on paper towels.
4. When cool, toss with parsley and parmesan cheese, and add them to your favorite salad.

Try this hot idea!

Chili Bagels

What you need

2 bagels, sliced in half horizontally
15-ounce can chili without beans

1 small onion finely chopped

$\frac{1}{2}$ cup sour cream

2 teaspoons chopped scallions (spring onions)

What you do

1. Toast bagel halves in toaster or oven.
2. While bagels are heating, heat chili in saucepan.
3. Spoon chili onto heated bagel halves, top with chopped onion and a heaping spoonful of sour cream.
4. Sprinkle chopped scallions on top. Makes 4 halves.

Alp yourself to a taste treat...

Swiss Bagels

What you need
2 bagels, sliced in half horizontally

$\frac{1}{2}$ cup mayonnaise

1 cup diced swiss cheese

1 tablespoon dried or fresh chopped parsley

4 slices dill pickle, optional

What you do
1. Mix mayonnaise, cheese, and parsley together.
2. Spoon onto bagel halves and bake in 375° oven on foil-covered cookie sheet for about 10 minutes or until cheese melts. Top each with dill pickle slice, if desired, before serving. Makes 4 halves.

Really good with pumpernickel bagel!

The Winner's Circle

What you need
1 bagel, sliced in half horizontally

1 hard boiled egg, sliced

2 teaspoons mayonnaise or salad dressing

1 lettuce leaf

salt and freshly ground pepper to taste

What you do
1. Spread mayonnaise or salad dressing on bagel halves.
2. Place hard boiled egg slices on bottom half, then lettuce leaf.
3. Sprinkle salt and pepper to taste.
4. Add top half of bagel. Serves 1.

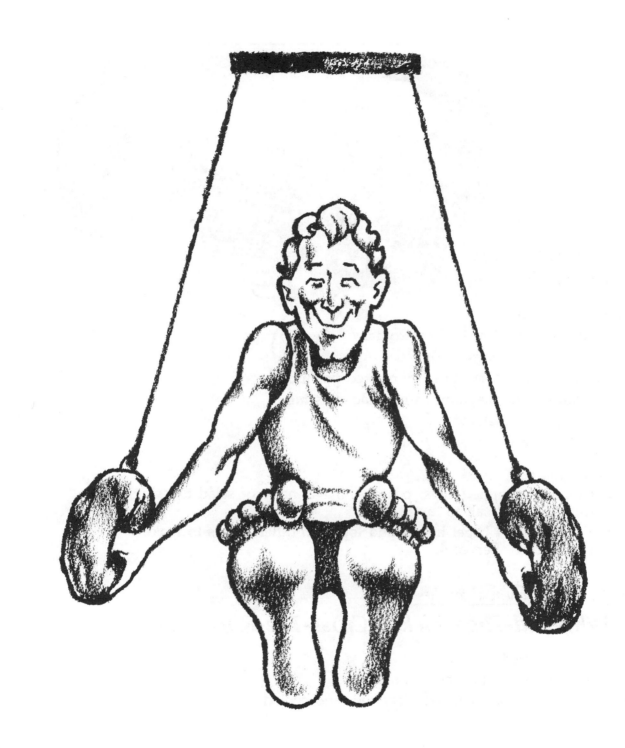

These are no yolk...

Eggsotic Bagels

What you need
4 bagels, sliced in half horizontally
4 hard-boiled eggs, chopped
$1/3$ cup chopped salt-free dry-roasted peanuts
4 tablespoons mayonnaise or salad dressing
$1/2$ teaspoon mustard
   salt to taste

What you do
1. Combine chopped eggs, peanuts, mayonnaise or salad dressing, mustard, and salt to taste.
2. Spoon onto 4 bagel halves and top with other halves to make sandwiches. Serves 4.

You'll cross any road for these!

Why-Did-The-Chicken-Cross-The-Road Bagels?

What you need
4 bagels, cut in half horizontally
4 chicken breasts cooked, deboned, and cooled

Krafts' Catalina® salad dressing or similar dark, sweet-spicy
French dressing

$\frac{1}{3}$ cup sour cream

8 water chestnuts (canned), finely chopped

salt and pepper to taste

What you do

1. Cut cooked chicken breasts in bite-size pieces.
2. Add enough salad dressing to coat lightly and thoroughly.
3. Mix in sour cream, water chestnuts, salt and pepper.
4. Spoon chicken salad on each of the bagel halves. Makes 4 halves.

Not for members only:

Club Bagel

What you need

1 bagel, cut in thirds horizontally, as shown

2 slices (2 ounces) turkey or chicken

2 slices corned beef

1 slice Muenster cheese

2 lettuce leaves

2 slices tomato

mayonnaise or salad dressing

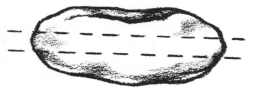

What you do

1. Spread mayonnaise or dressing on each layer.
2. Place turkey and cheese on bottom bagel layer.
3. Top with middle bagel layer and add lettuce, bacon and tomato.
4. Cover with top third of bagel. Serves 1.

Perfect for hearty appetites

Sloppy Bagels

What you need

3 bagels, cut in half horizontally

1 pound ground beef

1 medium onion, finely chopped

1/4 pound mushrooms, sliced thin

16 ounces bottled or canned spaghetti sauce

3/4 teaspoon salt

1/8 teaspoon pepper

1 celery stalk, chopped fine

What you do

1. Brown ground beef in large frypan with celery, onion, salt and pepper. Drain off fat.

2. Add spaghetti sauce and mushrooms to beef in frypan.

3. Simmer uncovered over low heat for about 10 minutes, stirring occasionally.

4. Toast bagel halves in toaster or oven. Spoon beef mixture onto bagel halves and serve. Makes 6 halves.

A fun—and yummy—hors d'oeuvre! Make this recipe up ahead and refrigerate or freeze before baking.

Inside-Out Bagels

What you need
  2 bagels, sliced in half horizontally
      dijon-style mustard
      mayonnaise
  2 tablespoons sweet pickle relish (be sure to drain off juice)
  2 large slices swiss cheese, each cut in 24 squares approximately 1'' each
20 slices of bologna, cut in halves
      toothpicks

What you do
1. Spread bagel halves with mustard and mayonnaise.
2. Top each with relish.
3. Cut each bagel half vertically into 10 bitesize pieces.
4. Place cheese square on each.
5. Wrap half slice of bologna around each bagel chunk and secure with toothpick.
6. Heat in 375° oven for 5 minutes. Makes 40 individual hors d'oeuvres.

Save much room for:

Mushroom Bagels

What you need
1 bagel, sliced in half horizontally
1 tablespoon margarine
1 cup chopped fresh mushrooms

$^1\!/_4$ teaspoon thyme

1 small onion, chopped

2 slices swiss or Muenster cheese

What you do

1. Saute mushrooms and onions in margarine, stirring in thyme.
2. Spoon mixture on bagel halves.
3. Top each with slice of cheese.
4. Bake on foil-covered cookie sheet in a 375° oven 8 to 10 minutes or until cheese melts. Makes 2 halves.

*Even if you **hate** cottage cheese, this tastes GREAT!*

Veggie Bagels

What you need

1 bagel, sliced in half horizontally

$3/4$ cup cottage cheese

$1/8$ cup radishes, very finely chopped

$1/8$ cup green pepper, grated

$1/4$ cup celery, finely chopped

$1/8$ cup carrots, grated

$1/4$ cup scallions (spring onions), finely chopped

salt and pepper to taste

What you do

1. Mash cottage cheese with fork and add radishes, green pepper, celery, carrots, scallions, and salt and pepper to taste.
2. Spread on bagel halves. Makes 2 halves.

Don't knock it 'til you've tried it.

The Wurst Bagel

What you need

1 bagel, sliced in half horizontally

1 good-sized cooked hotdog or knockwurst

$1/4$ cup sauerkraut, well drained

1 teaspoon sweet pickle relish, optional

mustard and catsup

What you do

1. Slice the wurst of your choice in half and then into thin strips.
2. Place on bottom bagel half.
3. Top with sauerkraut. Add relish, if desired.
4. Spread mustard and catsup on top half of bagel and place on top. Serves 1.

Steak your guests to

Bagel Mignon

What you need

   1 bagel, cut in half horizontally
   4 thin sandwich sub steaks, cooked according to package directions
   1 small onion, thinly sliced
   4 mushrooms, thinly sliced
¼ green pepper, thinly sliced
½ cup shredded mozzarella cheese
      small amount of cooking oil

What you do

1. Place 2 thin sandwich sub steaks folded in half on each bagel half.
2. In small amount of oil in frypan, cook onions, mushrooms, and green pepper slices until tender. Spoon mixture onto bagel halves.
3. Top with mozzarella cheese and put under the broiler until the cheese melts. Makes 2 halves.

It's the reel thing.

Catch-Of-The-Day Bagel

What you need

1 bagel, cut in half horizontally
2 fish sticks, cooked according to package directions
$\frac{1}{4}$ cup shredded and chopped raw cabbage, firmly packed
2 tablespoons mayonnaise or salad dressing
1 teaspoon sweet pickle relish

What you do

1. Heat bagel halves (optional).
2. Place cooked fish sticks on bottom half.
3. Mix together chopped cabbage, mayonnaise or salad dressing, and relish, and spoon onto fish sticks. Top with bagel half. Serves 1.

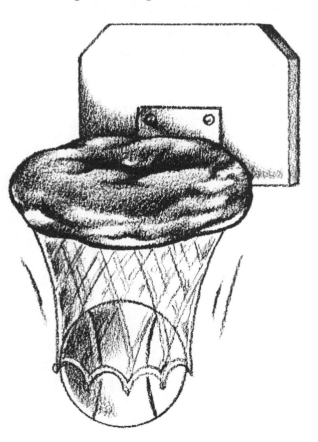

This is rich in vitamins, minerals, and protein. It will also start your taste buds humming!

Hummus Bagel

What you need
  2 bagels, sliced in half horizontally

     16-ounce can of chick peas (garbanzos), drained

½ cup of tahini sauce (sesame seed dressing —We use Telma®
     brand, which comes in an 11-ounce can.)

     analfa sprouts

     garlic powder to taste

What you do
1. Put drained can of chick peas in a blender or food processor and
   blend until smooth.

2. Add half-cup of tahini sauce and blend until completely mixed.

3. Add garlic powder to taste. You now have hummus.

4. Put heaping ¼ cup of hummus on each bagel half and top with
   alfalfa sprouts. Makes 4 halves.

If you've been timid about trying tofu, this is a great introduction! If you're a tofu fan, this is an unbeatable combination.

Tofu Bagel

What you need

   2 bagels, sliced in half horizontally
10 ounces tofu (soybean curd)
$\frac{1}{2}$ cup mayonnaise or salad dressing
   1 tablespoon Dijon-style mustard
$\frac{1}{2}$ teaspoon garlic powder
$\frac{3}{4}$ cup chopped celery
$\frac{3}{4}$ cup chopped green pepper
   1 small onion, chopped fine
   1 tablespoon soy sauce

What you do

1. Drain and mash tofu.
2. Mix with remaining ingredients and blend well.
3. Spoon $\frac{1}{4}$ of the mixture onto each bagel half. Makes 4 halves.

Chapter 9

Bagel Sweets and Treats
Ending on a Sweet Note

Tasting this is the next best thing to being in love! You'd butter make enough for everyone. . . .

Butterscotch Bagels

What you need
   2 bagels, cut in half horizontally
   4 teaspoons margarine or butter
1⅓ cups butterscotch chips
      2¼-ounce package salted cashew nuts, chopped

What you do
1. Spread each bagel half with a teaspoon of margarine or butter and place on foil-covered cookie sheet.
2. Put ⅓ cup of butterscotch chips on top of each buttered half.
3. Top with chopped cashews and bake in 375° oven until chips melt, about 15 to 20 minutes. Makes 4 halves.

You'll love these! They're heavenly! Use different kinds of pie filling to make an assortment of pastries. You can make these a day ahead or freeze them.

Bagel Cheese Pastries

What you need

4 cinnamon-raisin bagels, cut in half horizontally

8-ounce package cream cheese, softened (bring to room temperature)

$\frac{1}{4}$ cup granulated sugar

$\frac{1}{8}$ teaspoon cinnamon

2 teaspoons lemon juice

1 egg

1 teaspoon vanilla

20-ounce can cherry pie filling

What you do

1. With fingers, scoop out some of the insides of bagel halves to make shells. Freeze the bagel bits for other uses (like bread crumbs or poultry stuffing).
2. In mixing bowl, place softened cream cheese, sugar, cinnamon, lemon juice, egg, and vanilla. Beat very well so that all ingredients are thoroughly blended. Electric mixer is best.
3. Carefully spoon mixture into each bagel shell.
4. Bake on foil-covered cookie sheet in 375° oven for 15 minutes.
5. When cool, top each with a couple of spoonfuls of cherry pie filling. Makes 8 halves.

These are simply out of this world! If you have superior willpower, you can make them a day ahead.

Perfectly Pecan Bagels

What you need
 3 cinnamon-raisin bagels, cut in half horizontally
 3 eggs
$\frac{1}{2}$ cup brown sugar
 1 cup light corn syrup
$\frac{1}{8}$ teaspoon salt
 1 teaspoon vanilla extract
 1 tablespoon margarine or butter, melted
$\frac{3}{4}$ cup chopped pecans
30 pecan halves to garnish

What you do

1. Scoop out insides of bagel halves with fingers. Crumble the bits and set aside. You will have 6 "shells."
2. In mixing bowl, beat eggs and add brown sugar, corn syrup, salt, and vanilla. Beat well.
3. Add melted margarine or butter and blend.
4. Stir in chopped pecans and crumbled bagel bits; mix thoroughly.
5. Spoon mixture carefully into each bagel half and top each with 5 pecan halves.
6. Bake on foil-covered cookie sheet in 375° oven for approximately 25 minutes.
7. Transfer to a plate to cool or they will stick to the foil. Makes 6 halves.

Be sure to keep these refrigerated until you serve them. (It's also a good place to hide them from chocoholics) True chocolate lovers can use chocolate jimmies in place of coconut and nuts. Multi-colored jimmies are fun, too!

Evy's Chocolate Covered Bagel Chips

What you need

   bagel chips (make sure you DON'T get garlic, onion, pumpernickel, or rye-flavored)
12 ounces semi-sweet chocolate chips
 3 tablespoons cooking oil
   chopped nuts (walnuts or pecans)
   coconut

What you do

1. Put chocolate chips and oil in saucepan. Over low heat, stir constantly with wooden spoon until chips melt and mixture is blended thoroughly.
2. Keep saucepan on very low flame and put bagel chips in chocolate one at a time, turning to coat. Use wooden spoon to make sure both sides are thoroughly coated. Spoon off excess chocolate and place on wax-paper-covered cookie sheet.
3. When all the bagel chips are coated and on wax paper, sprinkle some with coconut and some with chopped nuts. Refrigerate until chocolate hardens. If you've used whole bagel chips, break into smaller pieces.

This makes enough to coat 14 bagel chips (whole pieces) or more if you're using broken pieces.

Satisfy your sweet tooth.

The Sugar Plum Bagel

What you need

 1 bagel, cut in half horizontally

$1/4$ cup damson plum preserves (try to get the "chunky" style)

$1/4$ cup slivered almonds
   powdered sugar

What you do

1. In small bowl, mix preserves with almonds.
2. Spoon half of the mixture onto each bagel half.
3. Sprinkle with powdered sugar before serving. Makes 2 halves.

This is wonderful with chocolate-chip or banana-nut bagels, if you can get them. For extra crunch, use sesame seed bagels. For chocolate-peanut butter fondue, use half chocolate chips and half peanut butter chips and eliminate almond extract.

Chocolate-Almond Bagel Fondue

What you need

   bagels, cut into bitesize chunks

 6-ounce package of semi-sweet chocolate chips

 2 teaspoons margarine or butter

$1/2$ cup table cream

$1/4$ teaspoon almond extract

What you do

1. Place chocolate chips and margarine in saucepan and begin melting over low heat.
2. As chips start to melt, gradually add cream, stirring constantly.
3. When chips have completely melted and mixture is blended, add almond extract and mix well.
4. Pour warmed mixture into fondue pot over low flame and serve with bite-size bagel chunks and fondue forks for dipping.

Outstanding!

Sno-Ball Bagels

What you need

1 cinnamon-raisin bagel, cut in half horizontally

2 5-ounce cans prepared vanilla pudding

1 cup thawed frozen non-dairy whipped topping

½ cup shredded coconut

What you do

1. Heat bagel halves just until warmed.
2. Spoon one 5-ounce can of vanilla pudding onto each bagel half.
3. Spoon ½ cup of non-dairy whipped topping over pudding.
4. Sprinkle each with ¼ cup coconut. Serves 2.

Easy and crunchy-good!

Choco-Peanut Bagels

What you need
bagels
canned ready-to-spread chocolate frosting
peanut butter, smooth or crunchy
chopped peanuts

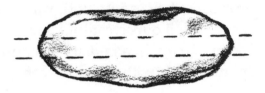

What you do
1. Cut each bagel in thirds, horizontally, so each has three layers as shown.
2. Spread bottom layer with peanut butter, then place middle layer on top and spread that with peanut butter.
3. Replace top. Then frost top with chocolate frosting and sprinkle on chopped peanuts.

*This is scrumptious as is, but if you want to go all the way add a small
scoop of ice cream or whipped cream!*

The Big Apple Bagel

What you need

 5 whole cinnamon-raisin bagels

21-ounce can apple pie filling

 1 cup flour (all-purpose or whole wheat graham flour)

$\frac{1}{4}$ cup soft margarine or butter

 2 tablespoons brown sugar

$\frac{1}{4}$ teaspoon cinnamon

What you do

1. Slice thin portion off the top of each bagel as shown, and with
   fingers scoop out inside to make a "shell." Freeze bagel bits and
   tops for later use.
2. Place $\frac{1}{2}$ cup pie filling in each bagel shell.
3. Place flour, soft margarine or butter, brown sugar, and cinnamon
   in a small bowl and mix with fork. Then crumble with fingers until
   thoroughly blended.
4. Spoon crumb topping over each apple-filled bagel, pressing crumbs
   onto filling. Bake on foil-covered cookie sheet in a 375° oven for 30
   minutes. Serve warm. Serves 5.

Keep this in the refrigerator for:

Going Bananas Over Bagels

What you need

cinnamon-raisin bagels, sliced in half horizontally

1 tablespoon honey

1 ripe banana, mashed

³/₄ cup whipped cream cheese

¹/₄ cup chopped pecans

What you do

1. Mix honey, mashed banana, and whipped cream cheese until well blended.
2. Use as spread on bagel halves or—better yet—dunk them into the dip. Makes 1 cup of spread or dunk.

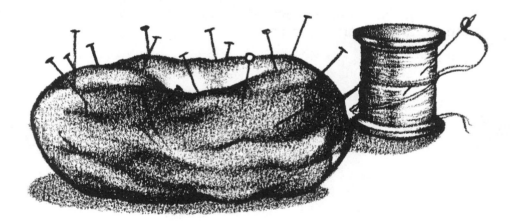

This tastes like cake! It's a delectable adult dessert that kids like too!

Bagel Rummy

What you need
4 very fresh cinnamon-raisin bagels, cut in half horizontally

2 pints rum-raisin ice cream

Rum Sauce:

$^1/_3$ cup soft margarine

1 cup brown sugar

2 tablespoons light corn syrup

$^1/_3$ cup table cream

$^1/_2$ teaspoon rum extract

(Makes approximately $1^1/_2$ cups sauce)

What you do
1. Heat bagel halves in oven until warm.
2. Remove from oven and immediately place a scoop of rum-raisin ice cream on each bagel half.
3. Top with warm rum sauce. Serves 8.

Prepare rum sauce by melting margarine over low heat. Stir in brown sugar, corn syrup, and cream, and bring to boiling. Remove from heat and stir in rum extract.

Delish!

Honey Dips

What you need
1 bagel, cut in half horizontally
  butter or margarine
  honey

What you do
1. Butter halves of bagel and cut each into quarters.
2. Heat in oven and then dip in small bowl of honey.

This varies with the berries

Berry Good Bagels

What you need
1 bagel, cut in half horizontally
  powdered sugar
1 cup blueberry, cherry, or strawberry canned pie filling
  whipped cream

What you do
1. Sprinkle cut side of bagel halves lightly with powdered sugar and heat them in oven until heated thoroughly.
2. Spoon ½ cup of pie filling on each half.
3. Top with generous helping of whipped cream. Serves 2.

We chose chocolate frosting but you can pick your favorite from flavors like chocolate chip, lemon, vanilla, coconut-pecan, and peanut butter cream, as well as all kinds of chocolate. Keep a can of frosting in the cupboard, and you're always ready to build:

Frosty The Bagel

What you need
  bagels, cut in half horizontally
1 can ready-to-spread chocolate frosting
  chopped walnuts

What you do
1. Frost cut side of bottom half of bagel.
2. Replace top half and spread frosting on top.
3. Sprinkle with chopped nuts or jimmies, and enjoy.

Best with a sweet bagel, like cinnamon-raisin bagels, banana nut bagels or—if you can find them—chocolate chip bagels.

Bagels Alaska

What you need
 1 cinnamon-raisin bagel, cut in half horizontally
 1 cup ice cream (your choice...we use butter pecan.)
$1/2$ cup miniature marshmallows
 2 tablespoons chocolate fudge topping or syrup

What you do
1. Preheat oven to 500° and prepare to work fast.
2. Put $1/2$ cup ice cream on each bagel half.
3. Press miniature marshmallows into ice cream.

4. Place on foil-covered cookie sheet and bake in 500° oven for 2 to 3 minutes until marshmallows lightly brown.

5. Remove from oven and top each with a tablespoon of chocolate fudge topping or syrup.

6. Serve immediately, with sharp knife and spoon or fork. Serves 2.

These are top notch! Prepare ahead and keep them in your freezer to bake when you want to serve a memorable dessert.

Coconutty Bagels

What you need
1 bagel, cut in half horizontally

$1/8$ cup shredded coconut

$1/8$ cup chopped walnuts

1 teaspoon brown sugar

$1/8$ cup soft margarine

1 tablespoon Heath® Bits O'Brickle almond brickle chips (optional)

What you do
1. Combine coconut, chopped nuts, brown sugar, and margarine.

2. Add Heath® Bits O'Brickle, if desired. Mix well.

3. Spread on bagel halves. Bake on aluminum foil in a 400° oven for 8 to 10 minutes. Cool for 5 minutes before serving. Makes 2 halves.

Fun and yummy!

Chewy Bagel Candy

What you need

1 bagel, cut in twelfths, vertically, as shown

$\frac{1}{4}$ cup plus 2 tablespoons chopped macadamia nuts

18 caramels

2 teaspoons water

What you do

1. Place caramels and water in saucepan and melt over low heat, stirring constantly.
2. As caramels start melting, add $\frac{1}{4}$ cup chopped macadamia nuts and continue stirring over heat.
3. Remove from heat and quickly spear bagel chunks with fork—one at a time—and dip into caramel-nut mixture until coated on all sides; place on wax paper. Work quickly so mixture doesn't harden. (If it does, you can reheat it over a low flame.)
4. When all pieces are coated, sprinkle with remaining 2 tablespoons of chopped nuts; press the nuts into the caramel coating.
5. Let cool and cover with plastic wrap. Makes 12 pieces.

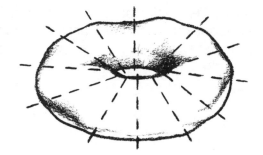

Serve with a Magnum (of champagne, of course)

Hawaii O-O

What you need
1 bagel, cut in half horizontally

$\frac{1}{2}$ cup whipped cream cheese

2 teaspoons brown sugar

$\frac{1}{4}$ cup chopped pecans

1 pineapple ring, finely chopped and drained on paper towels

2 whole pineapple rings, drained on paper towels

What you do
1. Combine whipped cream cheese, brown sugar, chopped pecans, and finely chopped and drained pineapple ring and mix thoroughly.
2. Spread onto bagel halves and top each with whole pineapple ring. Serves 2.

This can also be made with ricotta cheese (regular or low-fat part skim) instead of cream cheese.

You'll definitely lick the bowl on this one.

Cannoli Bagels

What you need
  1 cinnamon-raisin bagel, cut in half horizontally

  1 cup ricotta cheese (regular or low-fat part skim)

$1/4$ teaspoon vanilla extract

  1 tablespoon plus 1 teaspoon powdered sugar

$1/4$ cup semi-sweet chocolate chips

  1 tablespoon chopped citron (or the kind of mixed assorted chopped fruits used for fruit cakes)

  1 tablespoon chopped pistachio nuts or chopped slivered almonds

What you do
1. Place ricotta cheese in blender and blend for a few seconds or until creamy.
2. With spatula, scrape out blender and place ricotta cheese in mixing bowl.
3. Add vanilla and all of powdered sugar and mix well.
4. Chop citron or fruitcake fruit into small bits and add to ricotta together with chocolate chips. Blend well.
5. Place half the mixture on each bagel half and sprinkle with chopped pistachio nuts or almonds. Serves 2.

Chapter 10

Celebrity Bagels
What's what with how the
"Who's Who" like *their* bagels!

From the nation's capital to the movie capital, bagels receive rave reviews. We've heard them from notables in radio, TV, journalism, literature, music, entertainment, business, education, and sports. Here's what our bageluminaries had to say!

Jane Alexander

Jane Alexander, highly acclaimed stage, TV and film actress, is known for her memorable portrayals as Eleanor Roosevelt in the television production of "Eleanor and Franklin," as Dustin Hoffman's neighbor in "Kramer vs. Kramer," and for roles in the stage and screen versions of "The Great White Hope" among others. But Jane's love of bagels is no act!

"I eat 5 or 6 bagels a week! I had my first bagel in 1960 and my favorite kind is plain—with the hole! My favorite way of eating them is with my teeth. I've tried all kinds of bagels, but I like plain ones the best. The strangest way I've ever eaten bagels is with re-fried beans! Why do I like bagels? They're chewy and exercise my jaw line!"

Isaac Asimov

Isaac Asimov, "one of America's treasures," is one of the country's foremost science fiction writers and prolific author about everything, having authored over 300 books on an extraordinarily wide range of topics. When he's not penning a book, Mr. Asimov is most likely preparing a bagel.

"I've been eating bagels ever since I was a child. My favorite kind is a plain bagel, and I usually have one a week, preferably with lox and cream cheese. I like bagels because they taste so good. In fact, I'd like to do more with bagels, but I eat too much food as it is!"

David Brenner

David Brenner, well-known comedian who always performs to packed houses, enjoys relaxing with well-packed bagels.

"I love eating my bagels 1) with my hands 2) with thickly piled cream cheese and smooth peanut butter 3) with cream cheese and tuna 4) with cream cheese and crisp bacon. Especially on untoasted plain or pumpernickel bagels. I've been eating them since I was two months and three days old, and on a good week I eat between 2,500 and 3,200."

Joan Rivers

Joan Rivers, noted comedienne and talented actress, is never at a loss for words about bagels.

"I first started eating bagels when I was 20 minutes old. That's when I had a bagel and a Hershey bar! My favorite bagels are the ones with the hole in the center. I love all varieties. How many do I eat a week? I stop counting after Tuesday. My favorite way of eating a bagel is as a sandwich, filled with a pepperoni pizza. The strangest thing I've ever eaten on a bagel is a banana split. Why do I like bagels? They seem to like me. They go right to my thighs and just won't leave."

Jerry Buss

Jerry Buss, owner of the Los Angeles Lakers basketball team and real estate company executive, says that although it's baskets that count on the court, off the court it's bagels.

"I first started eating bagels 10 years ago. My favorites are raisin bagels, especially when they're toasted with butter or cream cheese at breakfast time with bacon and eggs. They taste so good that I have to limit myself."

Meredith Baxter Birney

Meredith Baxter Birney, talented actress and star of NBC's series "Family Ties," is also a spokesperson for Clairol. Her performing roles are in front of the camera, but her favorite roll is a bagel!

"I love garlic and onion bagels! I first started eating bagels about 30 years ago and find their shape wonderfully appealing. I have three a week when I'm working, but none when I'm not. My favorite way of eating them is toasted *very* crisp—black on the edges— with *scads* of butter. For me, the strangest thing I've ever had on a bagel is cream cheese. I guess the reason I haven't experimented more with bagels is that I'm inhibited!"

Dr. Joyce Brothers

Dr. Joyce Brothers is the noted psychologist, radio and TV personality, columnist, author, and business consultant whom millions of people— nationally and internationally—rely upon as the source of wisdom, common sense and practical advice. She was named in a UPI poll as one of the ten most influential women. If you have any doubt about the significant "roll" bagels play in childhood, listen to Dr. Brothers!

"I first started eating bagels as an infant. My favorite kind of bagel is plain, and I eat several every couple of weeks with cream cheese. Bagels are the best teething rings ever devised.   You can keep a small child

or infant who's old enough to sit up and grasp an object entertained and happy for longer than anything else.''

William Conrad

William Conrad, highly accomplished stage and television actor, producer, director and narrator, is also an acknowledged chili gourmet who thinks bagels are *really* hot stuff.

"I first started eating bagels at the tender age of 3. My favorite kinds are salt, poppyseed, pumpernickel, raisin, rye—any *water* bagel—*no* egg bagels! I try to hold down the quantity to a baker's dozen a week. Bagels are sooo good! My favorite way of eating bagels is to toast them, then spread with cream cheese and chives and fresh chopped Jalapeño peppers. The strangest thing I've ever eaten on a bagel is chili con carne with rattlesnake meat. Why haven't I experimented *more* with bagels? What a negative way to ask a question—I'm the best bagel experimenter on my block!!''

Phyllis Richman

Phyllis Richman, Executive Food Editor and famed restaurant critic for *The Washington Post,* is a bagel purist. Ms. Richman started eating bagels as soon as she had teeth, and she's been giving bagels critical acclaim ever since!

"My favorite kind of bagel is a *good* one. But I won't tell you how many I eat a week. That's top secret! Now as to *how* I like eating them. . . Is there any other way than with nova and cream cheese? You don't mess around with perfection! Why do I like bagels? That's like asking why I like breathing!''

Fred de Cordova

Fred de Cordova, well-known producer-director of NBC's "The Tonight Show," thinks bagels have star quality. For Fred it's "Lights!... Cameras!...Bagels!"

"Why do I like bagels? Because bagels like me. I entered puberty with a bagel. That's when I first started eating them, and now my week wouldn't be complete without at least one. I would have experimented more with bagels if it hadn't been for parental warnings. Bagels can be habit-forming!"

Phyllis Diller

Phyllis Diller, famous comedienne and popular entertainer, always packs the house with her repartee. Phyllis is never at a loss for words and her observations about bagels are no exception!

"Even the *thought* of bagels is an inspiration to me. I bet you didn't know that President Reagan was so gung-ho to get all the ethnic votes, he went into a deli and ordered a bagel. The waiter said, 'How would you like that?' Ronnie said, 'On rye.' Incidentally, my advice is never eat a day-old bagel. There is a day-old bagel someplace in this world with teeth in it—mine! By the way, did you hear about the new Bagel Diet? You just eat the holes."

Norm Crosby

Norm Crosby, one of America's favorite comedians and popular entertainers, has a way with words that's like no other. But ask Norm for a monologue on bagels and he gives it to you straight!

"I started eating bagels when I was very young! Also, I played with them as a baby. They're difficult to chew with no teeth! I eat at least a half-dozen a week, especially pumpernickel. And I like them toasted with cream cheese or open face with tuna fish and a slice of onion. Actually, I've tried *everything* on bagels—even mustard sandwiches—hot dogs, caviar (not together!) and often a pickle sandwich using bagels. I like bagels because they're quick to prepare, tasty and good for you! If these sensible reasons aren't enough, I like 'em 'cause they're *bagels* and maybe because I don't like anything square!!''

Mark Goodson

Mark Goodson, the epitome of the consummate innovative producer, has created many of the most memorable, successful, and classic TV game shows, past and present, including ''I've Got A Secret,'' ''Beat The Clock,'' ''The Price Is Right,'' and ''Family Feud.'' Mark has absolutely no difficulty answering questions about bagels!

''I ate my first bagel in Sacramento—that sounds like a title of a song—when I was about 10. My favorite kind of bagel is good old fashioned plain...with cream cheese (natch!) and smoked fishes (natch!). No matter how many bagels I eat, it's never enough. The strangest thing I've ever eaten on a bagel is caviar once, but I really haven't experimented because I'm conservative bagel-wise. I like bagels because I love crusty things, and the taste of a bagel is redolent of my youth.''

Heloise

Heloise, the trusted ''Dean of Household Hints,'' shares her millions of fans' suggestions in her widely read column which appears in newspapers from coast to coast. Heloise will tell you that you should always have bagels on hand, because no household is complete without some.

''Why do I like bagels? What's not to like!?! I first started eating bagels in Washington, D.C. as a child. My favorite is whole wheat and, though I eat none when I'm in Texas, I eat as many as I can when I'm in New York! I like my bagels with cream cheese, onion, and tomatoes, or peanut butter and cream cheese. Actually, *nothing* is too strange to put on a bagel.''

Larry King

Larry King, America's Favorite T.V. and Radio Talk Show Host, is a bagel eater since birth. He really knows what he likes. Besides, bagels don't talk back!

"Bagels have a taste all their own. They are perfectly named. They fill, they bring pleasure—they are *bagels*! I eat about five or six a week and especially like salt bagels. My favorite way of eating them is with lox and cream cheese. All others are frauds."

Ed McMahon

Ed McMahon, is the host of the popular syndicated program "Star Search," co-host of NBC's "TV's Bloopers & Practical Jokes," and famous TV personality on "The Tonight Show," NBC. What else would you expect Ed to say about his favorite bagel but "Heeere's onion!"

"Onion bagels are # 1 with me. I eat 3 or 4 a week. I first started eating bagels while in the service during World War II. My favorite way of eating them is toasted with peanut butter or cream cheese and lox. I haven't tried other combinations because of my inherent shyness. Why do I like bagels? Because they're delicious! What better reason?"

Marvin Mitchelson

Marvin Mitchelson, famed palimony and divorce attorney to the stars, says the splits he *really* likes to work on are two bagel halves.

"I've been eating bagels for over 40 years, and my favorite kind is pumpernickel. I usually eat from 2 to 5 a week and love them hollowed out with lox, onion, and whitefish, no cream cheese. The strangest combination I've ever had on a bagel is banana and cottage cheese. Why do I like bagels? The undefinable feeling of being Jewish."

Isadore "Skip" Pines

Isadore "Skip" Pines, President, Hebrew National Kosher Foods, Inc., has the word on bagels—and it's "salami."

"Like this recipe called a 'Hole In One' from our '25 Unorthodox Things To Do With a Hebrew National Salami.' Just slice an onion bagel, spread it with brown mustard and place several slices of salami on each half. Then broil open face till crisp, add tomato slices and serve with coleslaw on the side. That's *my* favorite bagel!"

John Moschitta, Jr.

John Moschitta, Jr. is the uniquely talented commercial personality who fast-talks his way into millions of American living rooms with his memorable Federal Express TV commercials among others. The faster John speaks, the more time he has to eat his bagels—nice and slow!

"You never forget your first bagel. I had mine on Tuesday, July 14th, 1957, at 10:07 a.m. My favorite kind is poppyseed, and I have two a week. The strangest combination I've ever had on a bagel is pineapple with spaghetti sauce. But my all-time *favorite* way of eating bagels is with chopped liver, turkey, coleslaw, Muenster cheese, lettuce and tomato. I call it the 'Mighty Mouth-full!' Bagels taste great *any* time and *any* way, plus you can always play ring-toss with them!"

Geraldo Rivera

Geraldo Rivera, controversial and widely viewed talk-show host, is well-known for his penetrating style and investigative reporting. Geraldo investigated his first bagel over 20 years ago and liked what he found.

"I started eating bagels around 1965 when I moved to New York after college. My favorite kind is poppyseed. I eat 2 or 3 a week, either toasted or untoasted with cream cheese and olives—olives in between the bagel and cream cheese. The strangest thing I've ever eaten on a bagel is not so strange at all—raisins. I'm very conservative about my culinary adventures so I haven't experimented more. Why do I like bagels? They are tastier, funnier, and more creative than plain bread. And they taste great with cream cheese and olives!''

Phil "the Scooter" Rizzuto

Phil "the Scooter" Rizzuto, one of the most popular Yankees of all time, is now broadcaster for the New York Yankees baseball team. When Phil rounds the plate, there's always a bagel on it.

''I eat at least a half-dozen a week! I've been eating bagels ever since 1937. My favorite kinds are salt and plain, with cream cheese, lox, and chive cheese. The strangest combination I've ever had on a bagel is jelly, bananas, and cream cheese. Why do I like bagels? They're the *best* especially in the morning and late evening.''

Duke Zeibert

Duke Zeibert, popular restaurateur of Washington's famed Duke Zeibert's Restaurant, favorite meeting place of newsmakers and celebrities, is the roll-model of a great bagel lover!

''I eat bagels every day of the week! Especially pumpernickel with cream cheese and mustard. I've been eating bagels for so many years now I can't recall. Bagels give me wisdom and strength. Let's face it. How else could I settle petty differences between the Chef, Pastry Chef, Roll Baker, and Head Waiter—and try to keep them all!''

Willard Scott

Willard Scott, NBC "Today Show" personality and TV host is the Nation's Capital's favorite son. According to Willard, the national radar weather map can pick up bagels from coast to coast.

''Today's forecast is a sesame seed bagel, my favorite kind! Take it from ol' Willard—bagels are the greatest. Especially sesame bagels piled high with cream cheese. I eat 'em every chance I get. Now, if I could only figure out how to grow bagels on my farm!''

Doc Severinsen

Doc Severinsen, famed concert artist, is music director of ''The Tonight Show'' Band on NBC-TV. Does Doc ever put down his trumpet for a bagel? You bet!

''My favorite bagel arrangement is ham on an egg bagel. I've found that bagels are not only high in food value, they're also useful for construction purposes.''

Artie Shaw

Artie Shaw, legendary clarinet virtuoso, bandleader and arranger, says that bagels have been music to his ears for years!

''I first started eating bagels sometime before—or during—the first Crusade. I love onion bagels, sesame bagels, plain bagels—any way at all, just so it's a bagel! How many do I eat? Oh, 6 or 8 a week. I usually have them toasted with butter. Why, is there some other way? I'm your basic straight-ahead bagel type—nothing strange, nothing kinky. Asking me *why* I like bagels is like asking why I like breathing air or drinking water. All bagels are good and good for you,. too. So what's not to like?''

Liz Smith

Liz Smith, widely read syndicated show biz columnist of the ''New York Daily News,'' knows bagels make good press—especially with cream cheese.

''I had never even *seen* a bagel until 1949 when I came to New York and had my first one. I've tried peanut butter on bagels, but haven't experimented more because I'm too gentile and cowardly. I love sesame bagels and would eat more of them, but I have to ration myself! My favorite bagel is toasted with *lots* of butter and cream cheese. Bagels are *delicious* and a challenge to eat!''

Abigail Van Buren

Abigail Van Buren, whose syndicated ''Dear Abby'' column and advice is read and followed by millions of devoted readers, advises you to eat at least one bagel every day.

''I've been eating bagels ever since I had teeth. My favorite kind is an egg bagel. I go on sporadic bagel binges and eat bagels every day for a week. Then I knock off for awhile. My favorite way of eating them is to slice a bagel lengthwise, toast it, and load on the butter and cream cheese! I've also enjoyed caviar on bagels—a very expensive frivolity indeed. But worth it! I haven't experimented more because I'm happy with my present mode of eating bagels. I love them because they're *delicious*. Why else?''

Wolfman Jack

Wolfman Jack, featured host of music shows on television and radio, syndicates his well-known radio program through his company, ''Audio Stimulation.'' Does Wolfman Jack love bagels? That's right, that's right, that's right!

''I first started eating bagels soaked in formula when I was 8 months old. My favorite kind of bagel is the one with a hole in the center. I eat $5\frac{1}{4}$ a week, and my favorite way of eating them is with a close friend. The strangest thing I've ever eaten on a bagel is oatmeal, and I'd experiment more with bagels but the good ones cost too much 'cause they have to be shipped to L.A. from New York! Why do I like bagels? Anything with a hole in it is worth eating.''

Your Bagel Diploma

Congratulations! You've earned it, so hang it up with Bagel Pride!

Marilyn & Tom Bagel's
Bagel U.

Bagelaureate

Presented to _____
Who has successfully completed The Bagel
Book and is hereby awarded a B. B. --
Bachelor of Bagelology Degree.

Index

NOTES

NOTES

NOTES

NOTES